EXCEPTIONALITY, *11*(3), 129-130

T0347593

PREFACE

Introduction to the Special Issue

It is a source of great pleasure to have been afforded the opportunity to guest edit this special issue of *Exceptionality* with a focus on mathematics for students with disabilities. In an effort to make this issue truly special and to provide a focus for researchers, classroom teachers, and curriculum specialists, the issue is devoted to a single topic, *division*. Division was selected because it is a topic about which there is (a) considerable controversy relative to its place in the school curriculum, (b) only scant research with respect to the developmental attainments of students with disabilities, (c) meager intervention research to validate curriculum and instructional practices, (d) little attention with respect to assessment of higher order outcomes, and (e) modest attention to the topic in preservice and inservice teacher preparation programs.

There exists a concern over the extent to which the time allocated to division in the school program is actually worth the effort. We believe that division is an essential component of the mathematics curriculum, particularly if one makes a distinction between *knowing* about division and *doing* division, and if one also assures students a chance to learn division at high levels of meaning and skill. For example, it is important for the student to understand division as integral to the factor-by-factor = product relationship of multiplication and to use this relationship to solve an extensive array of formula-driven problems in a topic such as science. Division has an additional role in the program for students with disabilities because it is a meaningful topic through which a wide variety of developmental needs such as language comprehension, cognitive development, and social–personal characteristics can be addressed.

It is hoped that the components of this special issue will be considered in preservice and inservice education programs. The great majority of teachers teach division exactly as they were taught when they went to school. Our experience with teachers is that they see little value in alternative algorithms, or alternative representations, or in attempting to modify the mathematics instruction to address the needs of students. Preservice and inservice education programs can provide the teachers with an alternative view of the mathematics they present to the students. The result of this is likely to be a higher quality of outcome for both the student and the teacher.

The articles in this issue discuss a number of curricula and instructional practices that have direct and meaningful implications for the classroom. Foley and Cawley discuss the general nature of the mathematics of division and stress the importance of providing the students with experiences that will enable them to both *know about* and be able to *do* division. Bryant, Hartman, and Kim discuss an explicit approach to math problem solving integrated with extensive use of teaching strategies. The Montague article describes a problem-solving or constructivist approach to division. Parmar describes an alternative framework for assessment, one that focuses on high quality outcomes and involves the student in a variety of ways to determine levels and types of knowledge and skill.

The articles in this special issue serve as a foundation for the development of research into effective intervention practices. This issue also provides an opportunity to extract selected features of instruction from the articles found herein, and to contrast the effectiveness of two distinct instructional approaches—constructivism and direct/-explicit instruction.

We hope to provide interested readers with an expanded view of division. We also trust this expanded view will prove beneficial in math instruction of students with disabilities.

John F. Cawley and Louise J. Cawley
Guest Editors

About the Mathematics of Division: Implications for Students With Disabilities

Teresa E. Foley and John F. Cawley
Department of Educational Psychology
University of Connecticut

The general purpose of this article is to highlight many of the components of the mathematics of division. These elements (e.g., identity elements, such as when a number is divided by 1, etc.) should be integral to any curriculum and instructional practice and they should be explicitly addressed to assure students an opportunity to learn. In highlighting these components, we differentiate between *knowing* about division and *doing* division. Our expectancy is that those who provide programming to students with disabilities will also recognize that programs in mathematics must address 2 factors. First, the program must assure that the students will attain high levels of competency in *knowing* about mathematics and in *doing* mathematics. Second, the program must utilize the principles, skills, and activities of mathematics to provide students with disabilities with experiences that will enhance their overall development in areas such as language comprehension, cognition, social-personal functioning, and independent strategy learning.

Informally, division is defined as the process of distributing the items in a single large set into multiple smaller sets, each of which contain an equal number of parts. At a more formal level, division may be conceptualized as the disunion of a single larger set into equivalent disjoint sets with or without a remainder (Reisman, 1977). Division is the inverse of multiplication as multiplication refers to a number of smaller sets of equal size that are grouped into a single larger set. The two processes can be viewed, Figure 1, as the distinctions between one-to-many and many-to-one relationships.

The two primary conceptualizations of division (e.g., *measurement* and *partitive* division) and an understanding of the four key terms (e.g., *dividend, divisor, quotient,* and *remainder*) comprise the building blocks of division. In *partitive* division a larger element is partitioned into a specified number of groups, but the size of each group is unknown.

Requests for reprints should be sent to Teresa E. Foley, PhD, Department of Educational Psychology, University of Connecticut, 24 Glenbrook Road, U-2064, Storrs, CT 06269–2064. E-mail: tef589@hotmail.com

(a)

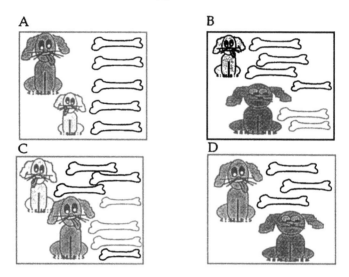

Basic Concept: Many-to-One
Look at the pictures. Point to the one where each dog has the same number of bones.
Answer: B

(b)

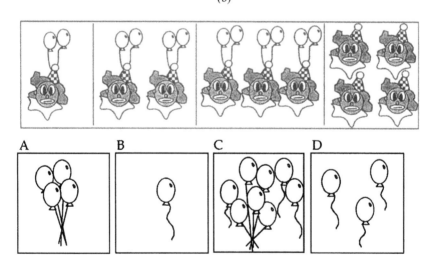

Basic Concept: One-to-Many
Look at the clowns. From the choices above, point to the picture that shows how many balloons
the last set of clowns should have.
Answer: C

FIGURE 1   Representation of one-to-many and many-to-one relationships.

Measurement division, on the other hand, refers to a situation where the size of each group is known but the number of groups is unknown. The four key terms refer to the number being divided (e.g., *dividend*), the divider (e.g., *divisor*) which represents the number of groups in *partitive* division and the number of elements in each group in *measurement* division, how many (e.g., *quotient*), and what is left over (e.g., *remainder*; Reisman, 1977).

Of the four arithmetic operations (i.e., addition, subtraction, multiplication, and division), division is the last to be introduced. This results in students receiving the least amount of formal classroom experience with division. Within the realm of computation, division is considered to be the most difficult of the arithmetic operations and typically has the largest number of prerequisite skills (Hatfield, Edwards, Bitter, & Morrow, 2000). This paper makes a distinction between *knowing about* division and *doing* division. As such, we suggest that students can be engaged in a variety of experiences to know about division as early as kindergarten.

COMPUTATIONAL DIVISION

There are many principles and understandings that students should know *about* division as well as many ways they can learn to *do* division. With respect to knowing *about* division, students should be able to explain, justify, and prove various meanings of division as well as the components of computation (e.g., search for a missing factor, many-to-one correspondence, etc.). When *doing* division students should understand concepts such as the missing factor (i.e., quotient) is found by dividing the known factor (i.e., dividend) by the divider (i.e., divisor). In addition, division can be represented in various formats and different algorithms can be used to carry out division calculations.

The primary purpose of this article is to highlight some of the important mathematical considerations in division to increase students' opportunities to know many things about division and learn different ways of doing division. This distinction of knowing about and doing division is necessary to encourage curriculum developers, districts, schools, and teachers to stress meaning about routines, applications, and connections over rote drill and practice. The selection of the full scope and sequence of division ought to be undertaken at the district and school level where the unique needs and characteristics of students should also be taken into consideration.

Some educational programs stress knowing and doing mathematics for its own sake. For example, students may learn prime numbers for intrinsic reasons or they may learn arithmetic computations because they are interesting, challenging, and valuable. Other programs stress the functional uses of mathematics and its applications in solving everyday problems related to social, family, or personal issues. In either case mathematics must do two things for students with disabilities. First, it must guide the students to learn important and meaningful mathematical concepts to high levels of proficiency. Second, it must assist the students to enhance their overall development in areas such as language comprehension, reasoning, creating and interpreting representations, communication, and social–personal development. With these points in mind let us look at a summary of the information on the general performance of students with disabilities and students considered to be normally achieving in division.

Figure 2 displays a set of single-digit speed-of-response data that provides a contrast between students with learning disabilities (SWD) and students considered to be normally achieving (SNA). Table 1 displays a set of data for single-digit through multidigit division items. In Figure 2 the data show that in grades 3 through 8, the rate of correct responses for SWD is approximately one-half that of SNA. In Table 1, the data for SNA show a continuous and steady growth in performance from smaller numbers to larger numbers. But the data also show some 35 to 55 percent of these students have not mastered division with larger number combinations by the age of 14. In addition, the data indicate that while lagging behind, the scores of the SWD approximate those of SNA. Such outcomes for SWD draws attention to the framework of the curriculum and its focus on making connections between what it means to divide, the mechanics of division, and when division is applied.

A CURRICULUM FRAMEWORK

We propose a curriculum framework for division that models a process structure which utilizes selected processes (National Council of Teachers of Mathematics, 2000) in teaching *about* division in contrast to only teaching students how *to do* division. It is suggested that the curriculum framework stress both *process* and *content* outcomes as seen in Table 2.

Efforts to align the curriculum with the needs and characteristics of students must recognize that the scope and sequence of traditional mathematics programs is unlikely to be achieved, on average, by students with disabilities. Available data indicate that the rate at which students with disabilities achieve is slower than that of students without disabilities

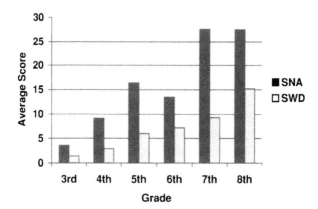

FIGURE 2 Automatization scores: Single-digit by single-digit division problems. SNA = Students considered to be normally achieving; SWD = Students with disabilities. N for SNA: grade 3 = 123, grade 4 = 132, grade 5 = 130, grade 6 = 114, grade 7 = 129, grade 8 = 109. N for SWD: grade 3 = 26, grade 4 = 35, grade 5 = 38, grade 6 = 39, grade 7 = 39, grade 8 = 20. Adapted from "Arithmetic Performance of Students: Implications for standards and Programming," by J. Cawley, R. Parmar, T. Foley, S. Salmon, S. Roy, 2001, *Exceptional Children, 67*(3), 311–328.

TABLE 1
Breakdown of Division Problems and Percentage of Students Responding Correctly

Age	4)$\overline{4}$ SWD	4)$\overline{4}$ SNA	4)$\overline{40}$ SWD	4)$\overline{40}$ SNA	4)$\overline{38}$ SWD	4)$\overline{38}$ SNA	4)$\overline{380}$ SWD	4)$\overline{380}$ SNA	4)$\overline{4060}$ SWD	4)$\overline{4060}$ SNA	6)$\overline{4060}$ SWD	6)$\overline{4060}$ SNA	46)$\overline{380}$ SWD	46)$\overline{380}$ SNA	44)$\overline{4060}$ SWD	44)$\overline{4060}$ SNA
9	00	51	6	4	00	4	00	4	00	4	00	2	00	2	00	2
10	18	20	9	00	9	00	9	00	9	00	9	00	00	00	00	00
11	00	85	6	56	00	59	00	44	00	37	00	37	00	26	00	15
12	70	91	52	78	48	81	52	75	48	69	39	59	17	44	9	16
13	82	97	65	78	47	83	53	86	35	81	59	67	29	75	18	64
14	100	100	100	73	67	85	67	73	93	92	60	77	67	73	40	54

Note. SWD = students with learning disabilities; SNA = students considered to be normally achieving. Adapted from "Arithmetic Computation Abilities of Students with Learning Disabilities: Implications for Instruction," J. Cawley, R. Parmar, J. Miller, & W. Yan, 1998, *Learning Disabilities Research & Practice, 11,* 230–237.

TABLE 2
A Schema for Stressing Content and Process in Division Instruction

	Process				
Content	Communication	Connections	Reasoning	Representation	Efficiency
Single Digit					
Multi-Digit					

and that their ultimate levels of attainment are 4 or more years below students for whom the general education curriculum is planned (Cawley, Parmar, Miller, & Yan, 1996, 1998). Thus, it is necessary that the curriculum framework be adjusted to focus on relevant and important mathematics and the integration of the processes by which students learn and demonstrate their knowledge *about* mathematics within their present level of functioning.

In this regard, students should have multiple opportunities to experience similarities and differences in contextual settings. For example, "times" should not solely be associated with multiplication. If given the problem, "Joshua has 27 apples. This is three times as many as he had when he started. How many apples did Joshua start with?" the students should not take the word "times" to suggest multiplication. The students need to be aware that determining the number of times "at bat" and the "times" of recess do not signal multiplication. Students need assistance and experiences to analyze contextual settings and they can only do this if sufficient instructional time is devoted to experiences in mathematics.

We have not focused on problem solving, per se, within the proposed framework because our thought is that problem solving should be an integral part of all aspects of mathematics and thus there is no need to single it out. For example, asking the students to do $3\overline{)12}$ and $5\overline{)20}$ or $2\overline{)8}$ and $2\overline{)6}$ fails to invoke a sense of problem solving. However, a slight modification of the task highlights a dimension of problem solving. For example, we can ask students to explain "Why is the answer the same to two very different problems?" in the first set of items, or "Why is the answer half the original amount in each problem?" in the second set of items. These types of questions encourage students to go beyond performing computations.

As an example, consider the common practice of having students do a page of eight, three-digit by one-digit division items (e.g., $3\overline{)156}$). The expectancy is that the students will provide a single acceptable response for each item and it may take them 20 to 30 minutes to complete the activity. The outcome is no comparison of the characteristics of the different items, no discussion of the procedures students use to complete the items, and no opportunity to use them in a meaningful manner. By contrast, consider a lesson that has only two, three-digit by one-digit items in which the students are asked to (a) complete the items, (b) describe the procedure or algorithm used, (c) complete the items again using a different algorithm, (d) describe the second algorithm used, (e) compare the two algorithms, (f) make a physical representation of the problem, and (g) explain why both algorithms work. These activities stimulate number sense and engage the students in knowing *about* mathematics (Gersten & Chard, 1999) as opposed to doing straight computations.

Learning *about* division means to recognize, explain, and prove selected meanings of the process of division. Some of these initial meanings are identifying the number of sets that can be created when each set has the same number of elements; finding the missing factor; partitioning, measurement, and division by 1 and 0; expressing the remainder as an integer or repeating decimal; division as a left-to-right operation; using alternative representations and algorithms; task and content analysis; and comprehending the nomenclature of division (i.e., dividend, etc.), curricula sequences, and formats used to represent division (e.g., $4 \div 2$, $2\overline{)4}$, ½). Higher-order outcomes for division would be attained when the students can demonstrate division as a many-to-one relationship, interchange between partitioning and measurement, and representing division as ratio. Given this array of basic understandings, discussions about division can be introduced long before computations with division can be initiated. Although an explanation of each is beyond the scope of this article, details are provided in a forthcoming book (Cawley, Foley, & Hayes, 2003).

For example, a kindergarten teacher could provide students with objects and ask them to put the same number of items in each of the four locations. The teacher could also request the students to "divide" the objects so that each of four locations has the same number of items. Sets of objects could also be displayed (e.g., Set 1 = xxx and Set 2 = yyyyyy), and students asked to determine the number of sets (i.e., when the size of the sets is known) or the size of each set (i.e., when the number of sets is known). Here the teacher can say, "See Sets 1 and 2, how many sets of objects (i.e., x's and y's, respectively) can you make if you put three objects in each set?" The students would count the number of items in Set 1 and indicate that only one set can be created (i.e., xxx). They would then count the number of items in Set 2 and indicate that two sets can be made because there are six items in the original set which can be separated into two sets of three items each (i.e., yyy; yyy).

The teacher could make another display (e.g., Set 3 = xxxx, Set 4 = yyyyyyyy, Set 5 = zz) and say, "See Sets 3, 4, and 5, how many sets of each object can you make if you put two objects in each set?" The students can count the number of sets of two x's in Set 3 and indicate that two sets can be made (i.e., xx, xx). They can then count the number of sets of two y's in Set 4 and indicate that four sets can be made (i.e., yy, yy, yy, yy). Finally they can count the number of sets of two z's in Set 5 and indicate that only one set can be made (i.e., zz). By engaging in this activity the students model division of a single digit divisor. They do so by simply exploring a relationship that helps them determine the number of groups of "objects" they can create if they start with a specified number of elements in each group. No symbolism or specific nomenclature is needed and no multiplication or subtraction is used. What the students learn is to model the language, "How many smaller sets can be made from an original set (e.g., xxxx, yyyyyyyy, zz) with a specified number of items (e.g., two) in each of the smaller sets." We will return to this model of division later in this article.

As part of their capacity to explain, the students could be asked: "What is the difference between these two sets of objects?"

Set 6	Set 7
XX	XXX
XXX	XXX
XXXX	XXX

The students would explain that the number of objects in the rows in Set 6 are not all the same, but they are the same in Set 7. The teacher could then provide the students with sets of objects (e.g., 16) and ask them to make sets in which the number of objects in each set are the same. Regardless of whether the students work independently or in small groups, they will likely produce different combinations (e.g., one student might produce two sets of eight, another student might produce one set of 16, etc.). The teacher could distribute another set of objects (e.g., 12) to the students and ask them to place 2 (or 1, 3, 4, 6, or 12) objects in each set to determine the number of sets they would create. The results of this activity could be compared with those of the previous activity and students could examine the similarities and differences between the outcomes. The teacher might then give the students another set of objects (e.g., 14) and ask them to make as many sets as they can, where each set has a different number of items. The outcomes of the three activities can be displayed and the students asked to compare the various arrangements relative to the computational processes they represent (e.g., addition, division). This provides the teacher with an opportunity to stress a major conceptualization of division, namely that different combinations of partitive and measurement division can be used by different students and regardless of which combination is used, each of the sets created by individual students has the same number of items.

Essentially, the students should differentiate situations in which they have a number of items and (a) distribute them so each of a given number of sets has the same number of items, (b) want to determine the number of sets that would result in a given number of items per set, and (c) create sets with varying numbers of items. These can be illustrated with word problems as follows:

- Huong has 10 apples and wants to give each of her 5 friends the same number of apples. How many apples will each friend get?
- Sean has 10 apples and wants to give each of his friends 2 apples. How many friends can Sean give apples to?
- Kadisha has 10 apples and wants to give some to each of her friends. If each friend gets one more apple than the friend before him or her how many of Kadisha's friends receive apples?

There are extensive opportunities in the classroom and in the natural environment to offer experiences that differentiate the partition and measurement contexts of division without even calling it division. For example, a given number of objects can be shared among students until all the objects are distributed. Depending on how the distribution was suggested, the students would use partitioning (e.g., give each of the six students the same number of crayons and determine how many crayons each student was given) or measurement (e.g., give 2 crayons to each student and tell how many students get crayons in sets of 2). This activity could be integrated with multiplication by asking the students to determine the total number of crayons for each distribution. The activity could also become a two-step activity. Assume there are 24 students in the class and the teacher indicates that each student is to be given 2 crayons. However, the teacher only has a total of 42 crayons, which results in some students receiving only 1 crayon or no crayons at all. The teacher could redirect the activity by asking the students for ways to determine the total number of crayons needed so that all students have two crayons. The recommendations generated by the students actively involve them as problem solvers in the instructional process.

Although these illustrations indicate that students understand the meanings of division, higher-order outcomes require us to take the students further with respect to the divisional process. We begin by identifying the prerequisite knowledge and skills that students need to successfully learn about and do single-digit division (e.g., $2\overline{)6}$). Prerequisite skills for single-digit division include the ability to interpret both spoken and written number symbols (e.g., "three" = xxx vs. 3 = xxx, etc.); count by 1s; do skip counting; understand one-to-one, one-to-many, and many-to-one relationships; and read the facts tables. Once students possess these understandings they can then engage in learning about and doing division. We begin with an illustration of the traditional algorithm where students are taught and apply selected principles of doing division.

Capitalizing on Single-Digit Division

Single-digit division provides numerous opportunities for students to interact with the mathematical process and explore a variety of features within this process. For example, we can show the students one or two exemplars and ask them to produce as many items as they can that are like the exemplar. To illustrate, let's consider $4\overline{)8}$ and $3\overline{)6}$, "See these two items. Make as many as you can that are like the ones shown." The scoring for this activity can follow the general model of creative thinking and include (a) frequency, or number of items produced; (b) divergency, or the number of different items produced; and (c) originality, or the number of items that are unique to each student compared to other students.

Students can engage in the process of evaluative thinking that requires analysis and judgment of which members of a group are "better" than others. Given $4\overline{)8}$ and $3\overline{)6}$, the students are asked to select the one which, in their opinion, is a better representation of division. There is no single correct response except in the reasoning the students use.

The students can be asked to contrast varying number combinations. For example, given $2\overline{)4}$, $4\overline{)8}$, and $6\overline{)12}$, the students can be asked to explain and justify why all of the problems have the same answer. Or, when given $3\overline{)6}$ and $3\overline{)9}$, the students can be asked to explain and justify why they have different answers.

Students can be shown the following items (i.e., $36 \div 2 = \_\_ \div \_\_ = \_\_ \div \_\_ = 3$ and $48 \div \_\_ = \_\_ \div \_\_ = \_\_ \div \_\_ = 4$) and asked to complete each item. A few students can be asked to write their items on the board. Each of the students is likely to have different combinations of numbers that satisfy the problem. These can then serve as the basis for a discussion about the variability in which students think about division.

The students can be presented with sequencing tasks and asked to complete the following sequences (i.e., $2\overline{)4}$, $2\overline{)5}$, $2\overline{)6}$, $2\overline{)7}$, ____; $4\overline{)5}$, $5\overline{)6}$, $6\overline{)7}$, $7\overline{)8}$, ____; $6\overline{)12}$, $5\overline{)10}$, $4\overline{)8}$, $3\overline{)6}$, ____; and $2\overline{)4}$, $3\overline{)6}$, $4\overline{)8}$, $5\overline{)10}$, ____). There are actually many more activities that can be utilized with single-digit combinations to build conceptualizations and skills with division, but space limits the presentation to these here.

In much of our own work, we utilize a framework for presenting alternative representations of mathematics principles and procedures. This framework is referred to as the Interactive Unit and consists of four categories of organizing information presented to the students (i.e., input) and four categories by which the students can respond (i.e., output), as shown below:

	Input			
Output	*Manipulate*	*Display*	*State*	*Write*
Manipulate	1	2	3	4
Identify	5	6	7	8
State	9	10	11	12
Write	13	14	15	16

On the Input dimension the term *manipulate* stipulates that the teacher moves, arranges or compiles two- or three-dimensional materials to represent a mathematical meaning or skill; *display* indicates that the teacher shows the students a fixed picture of an object which represents a mathematical meaning or skill. Outputs generated by students include *identify* which asks the students to simply point to a response; *state* calls for oral communication; and *write* indicates the use of written symbols consisting of letters, numerals, or other mathematical symbols. Ten of the 16 combinations (i.e., cells 2, 4, 5, 6, 7, 8, 13, 14, 15, & 16) can be used to create numerous worksheet formats. Figure 3 illustrates the write/identify combination.

Alternative Algorithms

The traditional approach to dividing $4\overline{)248}$ describes the process as "4 into 2 does not go, so we move over." In a meanings oriented context, the students would question this by saying something like, "I don't understand. If the 2 represents 200, why doesn't 4 go into 200?" Other students might pose a situation in which they say: "If the 4 won't go into the 2 how would you do it if it was written this way $4\overline{)200 + 40 + 8}$?" Telling the students that "4 does not go into 2 (200)" seems to violate all that we have taught the students with respect to place value. We do not argue that if the only purpose for teaching students *to do* division is to have them perform rote routines, then "4 into 2 does not go" could be used. We argue only that it is improper if one is teaching students to understand multiple ways of doing and representing division.

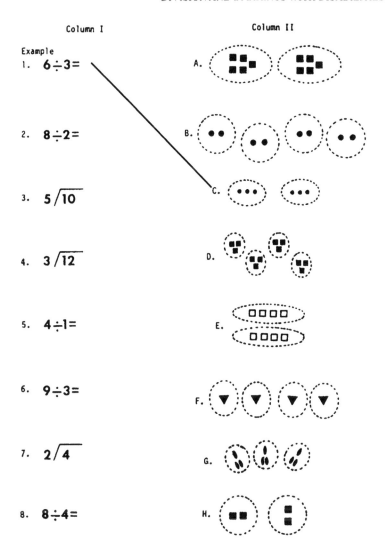

FIGURE 3 Worksheet activity on write/identify combination in the Interactive Unit.

It is likely that the great majority of students do not know how to use alternative representations of the operations. It is also likely that most students do not know how to do alternative algorithms. The significance of alternative algorithms is that they enhance the students' *sense of number*. With respect to $4\overline{)248}$ we describe two algorithms that have long been a part of arithmetic learning. The Greenwood and Pyramid algorithms directly below present alternative representations of division and are used as organized formats for the repeated subtraction concept imbedded in division (Laing & Meyer, 1982).

Pyramid	Greenwood	
62		
2 (2 times 4 = 8)		
10 (10 times 4 = 40)		
50 (50 times 4 = 200)		
4)248	4)248	
200	200	50 (50 times 4 = 200)
48	48	
40	40	10 (10 times 4 = 40)
8	8	
8	8	2 (2 times 4 = 8)

Each algorithm recognizes that the question being asked relates to the number of sets of 4 to be found in 248. Both algorithms require that students know, understand, and accurately apply place value and estimation. Assume the students have been organized into two small groups and have been asked to make alternative representations of 4)248. Group 1 indicates it will prepare a manipulative representation of the item and group 2 chooses to prepare a symbolic representation. The groups proceed as follows:

Group 1.   The group obtains a set of tongue-depressor sticks and arranges them to show eight 1s, four 10s in the form of four sets of sticks with each set having 10 individual sticks, and two 100s with each being composed of 10 sets in which each set has 10 individual sticks. The group displays the problem as shown in Figure 4 and poses the question, "How many sets with this many in each set [point to 4] can we make here [point to #s (100s)]." The answer is "none" because we only have two ## and we need at least four to make a set. This requires that the two 100s (i.e., #s) be regrouped to twenty 10s (i.e., *s) and combined with the existing 10s to make twenty-four 10s (i.e., #s). The question can then be asked, "How many sets with this many [point to 4] can be made here [point to *s (10s)]?" The students can encircle each set of 4, count the number of sets of 4 and record the number as shown. What remains is to determine "the number of sets here [point to +s (1s)] with this many in each set [point to 4]." Again, the students can encircle the number of sets with 4 in each set. Note that the only arithmetic the students used was counting; no multiplication or subtraction was involved.

Group 2.   The second group uses expanded notation to create a symbolic representation of the item as shown in Figure 4. Because the expanded notation is similar to the manipulative format, the procedure is the same for each. The question asked is "How many sets with this many in each set [point to 4] can be made here [point to the 100s]?" The answer is "none" because there are only two 100s and you need 4 to make at least one set. Similarly, the 100s are renamed as 10s and placed in the 10s column. Students are then asked to encircle each set with this many in each set [point to 4] and record the number of sets circled [point to 6]. What remains is to determine the number of sets with 4 in each set for the 1s column and here the students encircle the sets as shown and record the number [point to 2]. What has happened is that the students focus on division as a process to determine the number of items in each set or the number of sets with a given

Group 1:

$4\overline{)\#\#*\!*\!*\!*\!+\!+\!+\!+\!+\!+\!+}$ Where # = 100, * = 10, + = 1. After exchanging the #s for *s the problem becomes $4\overline{)*\!+\!+\!+\!+\!+\!+\!+\!+}$ which can be grouped into sets of 4 as follows:

So the answer is 6 sets of 10 and 2 sets of 1, which is equivalent to 62.

Group 2:

$4\overline{)100,100+10,10,10,10+1,1,1,1,1,1,1,1}$ After exchanging the 100s for 10s the problem becomes $4\overline{)10,10,10,10,10,10,10,10,10,10,10,10,10,10,10,10,10,10,10,10,10,10,10,10,10,10,10,+1,1,1,1,1,1,1,1}$ which can be grouped into sets of 4 as follows:

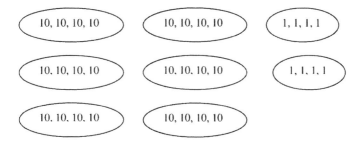

So the answer is 6 sets of 10 and 2 sets of 1, which is equivalent to 62.

FIGURE 4   Graphical and symbolic representation of division.

number of items. The focus is not on the traditional division algorithm where the students direct more attention to how to do division than to the meaning of division.

The illustration shows that the integrity of place value is maintained with both manipulative and symbolic representations. The two illustrations also show that the students can do division without the use of multiplication or subtraction. This provides an excellent opportunity for teachers to involve *all* students in a meaningful lesson on division, regardless of their mastery of multiplication or subtraction.

Division as Ratio

Ratio is an important principle of mathematics, yet students often have a difficult time with this concept. This difficulty might be attributed to the rote manner in which it is often taught or the failure to assist the students to recognize ratio as something common to their everyday world. In working with one-to-many or many-to-one relationships, students are engaged with ratio on a daily basis. That there are five fingers on each hand, five toes on each foot, two ears on each head, that a nickel equals five pennies, two nickels equal a dime, and ten dimes equal a dollar are all instances of ratio. The scale drawing for a house where one-fourth of an inch equals one foot, or 16 ounces make a pound, or 3 feet make a yard are additional illustrations of ratio. In effect, ratio expresses a part–whole relationship that can be expressed as $\frac{1}{3}$, 1:3, or "1 to 3" and is most often expressed in fractional notation (i.e., $\frac{1}{3}$). What may make the concept of ratio difficult for many students is that it is often introduced as something we do by dividing one number by another, "divide the numerator by the denominator," which we then express as a percent. This is more cumbersome than is necessary, so let us take a different approach.

Students' experience with ratio as a relationship between two numbers can begin when they are young. The concept of one-to-one correspondence where students learn to match each item in one set with an item in another set and then graduate to match one item in a set with more than one item in another set are both examples of ratio relationships. In the former, students are asked to show one doll for every doll carriage or draw one fish for every fish bowl. In the latter, students are asked to draw three apples on every tree or four tires on each truck. For students in the upper-elementary grades the exploration of ratio can be expanded to interpreting charts and illustrations where students are given activities with information presented in the form of charts or tables. As students master division, they begin to see that it essentially represents a stable relationship between two numbers.

Task and Content

We make a distinction between the tasks required from students and the content in which the students are to perform the tasks. What is often referred to as *task analysis* is actually not task analysis at all, but content analysis. Figure 5 shows a content list for division, which begins with single-digit items and proceeds to multidigit items in which the specific components of each item are identified in the sequence.

Throughout this content listing, the students perform essentially the same task. They follow the same rules and use only symbolically driven rote routines. They do not use alternative algorithms nor do they use alternative representations to communicate and reason with the mathematics. There is no designation of the cognitive acts the students might become engaged in nor are there any instances to show connections between or among mathematics principles (e.g., the relationship between multiplication and division).

Reality suggests it is inefficient and in some settings ineffective to work with large numbers such as four-digit-by-four-digit items simply because they are too bulky. Lessons involving items with larger numbers should include only two or three items. Students should be provided with ample time to do the items and then describe and discuss their procedures. The need is to determine that the students know how to do the

Item	Description	Example	Rename	Remainder	Zero
D1	One digit by one digit	3)9	No	No	No
D2	One digit by one digit	3)7	No	Yes	No
D3	Two digit by one digit	2)14	10s	No	No
D4	Two digit by one digit	3)26	10s	Yes	No
D5	Three digit by one digit	3)936	No	No	No
D6	Three digit by one digit	4)164	100s	No	No
D7	Three digit by one digit	5)163	100s & 10s	Yes	No
D8	Three digit by one digit	4)480	No	No	1s
D9	Three digit by one digit	3)603	No	No	10s
D10	Three digit by one digit	7)504	100s & 10s	No	10s
D11	Three digit by one digit	5)200	100s	No	10s & 1s
D12	Two digit by two digit	12)48	10s	No	No
D13	Two digit by two digit	16)51	10s	Yes	No
D14	Three digit by two digit	16)486	100s	Yes	No
D15	Three digit by two digit	26)734	100s & 10s	No	No

FIGURE 5   Content analysis for division.

items and that the conceptual bases for the items are understood. Once it is certain the students understand the meanings of division, are able to communicate about division, and show connections and demonstrate that they are quick and efficient in dividing smaller items, then they can use calculators to work with larger items.

Arithmetic Word Problem Solving

The conceptualization of arithmetic word problem solving from which we function is that word problem solving is a combination of language comprehension and information processing (Cawley, Foley, & Parmar, 2003a, 2003b). The problem-solving performance of students with disabilities from grades 3 through 8 is less than satisfactory, as indicated in Figure 6. The students make numerous qualitative errors such as including extraneous information when it should be excluded and being foiled by a mathematics term such as "divide" when the "divide" in the text does not mean divide.

What seems to happen is that the students fail to attend to the context in which words and information appears. Some of this may be due to difficulties with language comprehension, or information processing. As such, the primary source to which we direct your

Direct Problems without Extraneous Information

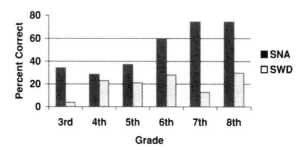

Direct Problems with Extraneous Information

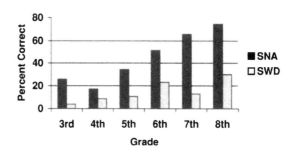

FIGURE 6   Average percent correct for arithmetic problem solving in division. SNA = Students considered to be normally achieving; SWD = Students with disabilities. N for SNA for grades 3–8 = 35; and for SWD for grade 3 = 26; grade 4 = 35; grade 5 = 38; grade 6 = 39; grade 7 = 39; and grade 8 = 20. Adapted from "Word Problem-Solving by Students With and Without Disabilities," by R. Parmar, J. Cawley, & R. Frazita, 1996, *Exceptional Children, 62*(5), 415–430.

attention is the text of the problem. The text may be presented in the form of written sentences, charts, tables, manipulatives, pictorial displays, or as oral statements. We give only minor attention to the question and to the inclusion of key words (e.g., divide). For example:

- Kimoy wanted to divide his apples so that each of his 4 friends got 3 apples. How many apples did Kimoy start with?
- Crystal wanted to distribute her apples so that each of her four friends would get the same number of apples. She has 24 apples, which is 2 times more than she needs. How many apples does Crystal need? How many apples will each of her friends receive?

With respect to division and the relationship between computation and problem solving, our sense is that the most important computational principle for students to master is the "factor × factor = product" relationship. That is, students must know how to exchange the components of this principle among related mathematical statements (e.g., $2 \times 5 = 10, 2 \times \_\_ = 10, \_\_ \times 5 = 10$ and $10 \div 5 = 2, 10 \div 2 = 5$). The reason for these examples is that a significant number of word problems, which students encounter, involve division that is embedded in formula-type problems such as "distance = rate × time" [e.g., $d = rt$].

- Rocky ran a distance of 10 miles in 2 hours. If he ran the same distance each hour, how many miles did he run each hour?
- Xin ran a distance of 10 miles at a rate of 5 miles per hour. How many hours did it take her to run the 10 miles?

Students with disabilities seldom make computational errors on problems of the type illustrated, especially when small numbers are incorporated in the problems (Glover, 1993). Their errors are typically related to the context of the problem in that they do not know the content material (e.g., they do not know *rate, time,* and *distance*). To build on students' understanding of the content material the two previous problems can be modified as follows:

- Octavio ran 2 miles in 5 hours. If Estella ran at the same rate for 6 hours, how many miles would she run?
- Joy ran 4 miles in 10 hours. If Max ran at the same rate for 5 hours, how many miles would he run?

Division is driven by formulas such as $d = rt$ across different subjects. The use of many of these formulas occurs in laboratory experiments, group projects, and individual problems. Some of these require the students to collect, process, and tally data and then adapt the data for use in various situations. For example, a common application for division is found in determining averages. This generally involves two-step problems where the students must first find a total and then divide the total by the number of incidents. Let us consider a few illustrations of formulas such as the following: momentum = mass × velocity, $(M = mv)$;   work = force × distance, $(W = Fd)$;   density = mass ÷ volume, $(d = \frac{m}{v})$; and pi = circumference ÷ diameter, $(\pi = \frac{C}{d})$. The actual level of the arithmetic computation can be controlled in problems so as not to over burden the students. In the formula $(\pi = \frac{C}{d})$, assuming $d = 8$ in., the components can be restated as $(C = \pi d)$, thus multiplying 8 and 3.14 to approximate the circumference as 25 in.; or $8\overline{)25}$ to approximate π; or $(d = \frac{C}{\pi})$ to approximate the diameter. Actual measurements can also be obtained by providing the students with circular-shaped objects and measuring tape and having them measure the circumference and diameter of the objects. Division is more than a routine that students learn in school, it is a dynamic process in which students interact with a variety of meanings and adaptations of processes to solve problems and establish connections with different areas of mathematics or other subjects.

SUMMARY

The illustrations of division highlight selected aspects of how the treatment of a single topic can enhance a program of mathematics for students with disabilities. Once the important mathematics have been selected, the teachers and staff should outline a "less-is-more" approach to provide students with in-depth understandings, meanings, and proficiencies in mathematical skills. A distinction between teaching *about* mathematics and teaching *to do* mathematics needs to be made, yet a balance between learning *about* and learning *to do* is essential for daily living. A number of curriculum and instructional guidelines at various structural levels are evident.

- Teachers, schools, and districts should work together to determine the important mathematics for *all* students and the components that will be stressed for students with disabilities.
- The selection of the mathematics to be incorporated into the curriculum needs to be partially guided by knowledge of the developmental levels of students with disabilities.
- The important principle of "less is more" should be used to guide the selection of activities and the grade levels when the activities will be presented.

Teaching *about* mathematics can be integrated into one or more instructional models and teachers can vary their instructional practices according to the level of meaning and proficiency they seek with their students.

REFERENCES

Cawley, J. F., Foley, T. E., & Hayes, A. M. (2003). *Whole numbers computation and problem solving for students with difficulties in mathematics*. Cambridge, MA: Brookline Books, Inc. Manuscript submitted for publication.

Cawley, J. F., Foley, T. E., & Parmar, R. (2003a). Expanding the agenda in mathematics problem solving for students with mild disabilities: Suggestions for method and content. Manuscript submitted for publication.

Cawley, J. F., Foley, T. E., & Parmar, R. (2003b). Further expanding the agenda in mathematics problem solving for students with mild disabilities: Alternate representations for problems. Manuscript submitted for publication.

Cawley, J., Parmar, R., Foley, T., Salmon, S., & Roy, S. (2001). Arithmetic performance of students: Implications for standards and programming. *Exceptional Children, 67,* 311–328.

Cawley, J., Parmar, R., Miller, J., & Yan, W. (1996). Arithmetic computation abilities of students with learning disabilities: Implications for instruction. *Learning Disabilities Research & Practice, 11,* 230–237.

Cawley, J., Parmar, R., Miller, J., & Yan, W. (1998). Arithmetic computation performance of students with learning disabilities and students who are normally achieving: Implications for curriculum. *Learning Disabilities Research & Practice, 13,* 68–74.

Gersten, R., & Chard, D. (1999). Number sense: Rethinking arithmetical instruction for students with mathematical disabilities. *The Journal of Special Education, 33,* 18–28.

Glover, M. (1993). The effect of the hand-held calculator on the computation and problem solving achievement of students with learning disabilities. Unpublished doctoral dissertation, State University of New York at Buffalo.

Hatfield, M., Edwards, N., Bitter, G., & Morrow, J. (2000). *Mathematics methods for elementary and middle school teachers* (4th ed.). New York: John Wiley & Sons.

Laing, R., & Meyer, R. A. (1982). Transitional division algorithms. *Arithmetic Teacher, 29*(9), 10–12.

National Council of Teachers of Mathematics (2000). *Principles and standards for school mathematics.* Reston, VA: Author.

Parmar, R., Cawley, J., & Frazita, R. (1996). Word problem-solving by students with and without disabilities. *Exceptional Children, 62,* 415–430.

Reisman, F., (1977). *Diagnostic teaching of elementary school mathematics.* Chicago: Rand McNally College Publishing.

Using Explicit and Strategic Instruction to Teach Division Skills to Students With Learning Disabilities

Diane Pedrotty Bryant, Paula Hartman, and Sun A. Kim
Special Education Department
The University of Texas at Austin

Students with mathematics learning disabilities (LD) exhibit difficulties with retrieval and cognitive skills that impede their ability to perform basic mathematical skills. Instruction in mathematical procedures (i.e., procedural knowledge) is necessary to help students learn and apply skills such as basic facts and whole-number computation. Division is a skill that is identified in curriculum across the grade levels; yet, it is a skill that is often taught last in instructional sequences because of its complexity and prerequisite knowledge. Reviews of research have revealed that students with LD benefit from a combined model of academic instruction that includes both explicit and strategic instructional procedures. This article presents an overview of division instruction and a sample of interventions for teaching division that include explicit and strategic instructional procedures, which are found in the combined model of teaching.

It is estimated that between 5% and 8% of school-age students exhibit memory or cognitive deficits that impede their ability to acquire, master, and apply mathematical skills and concepts (Geary, in press). Many of these students are identified as having mathematics learning disabilities (MLD). For example, studies with students who have MLD have identified differences in memory retrieval (Garnett & Fleischner, 1983; Jordan, Levine, & Huttenlocher, 1995) and strategic processes (Geary, 1990) that impede their ability to solve simple computation, basic facts, and word problems compared to the math abilities of typically achieving peers. In another study (Bryant, Bryant, & Hammill, 2000), special education professionals evaluated the performance of students with identified learning disabilities (LD) and math weaknesses ($n = 870$) compared to students with LD and no math weaknesses ($n = 854$) on a rating scale of math behaviors drawn from the research literature. Results indicated significant differences between the two groups on basic skills that contribute

Requests for reprints should be sent to Diane Pedrotty Bryant, Special Education Department, University of Texas–Austin, College of Education, Office of the Dean S2B 216, 1 University Station D5001, Austin, TX 78712. E-mail: dpbryant@mail.utexas.edu to students' ability to engage in and solve successfully higher order mathematical problems. Additionally, results from the study produced a ranking of math skills that were identified as most problematic for students with LD and math weaknesses. Inspection of these skills reveals difficulties with basic procedural knowledge that relates to memory and cognitive abilities, automaticity, and the language of mathematics (see Table 1). Thus, because students with MLD tend to exhibit persistent difficulty in learning and applying mathematical skills such as basic facts and whole-number computation, including division, instruction in basic mathematical procedures (i.e., procedural knowledge) is critical.

The focus of this special series is on *division*. Cawley and Foley (2003) describe division as the "process of distributing the items in a single large set into multiple smaller sets, each of which contain an equal number of parts." In reviewing state standards (e.g., California, Texas, New York) for mathematics curriculum, the teaching of division skills and concepts is evident across the grades. Table 2 provides a sample of curricula across

TABLE 1

Ranked Mathematical Difficulties Exhibited by Students With Learning Disabilities and Math Weaknesses

- Has difficulty with word problems
- Has difficulty with multistep problems
- Has difficulty with the language of math
- Fails to verify answers and settles for first answer
- Cannot recall number facts automatically
- Takes a long time to complete calculations
- Makes "borrowing" (i.e., regrouping, renaming) errors
- Counts on fingers
- Reaches "unreasonable" answers
- Calculates poorly when the order of digit presentation is altered
- Orders and spaces numbers inaccurately in multiplication and division
- Misaligns vertical numbers in columns
- Disregards decimals
- Fails to carry (i.e., regroup) numbers when appropriate
- Fails to read accurately the correct value of multidigit numbers because of their order and spacing
- Misplaces digits in multidigit numbers
- Misaligns horizontal numbers in large numbers
- Skips rows or columns when calculating (i.e., loses his or her place)
- Makes errors when reading Arabic numbers aloud
- Experiences difficulties in the spatial arrangement of numbers
- Reverses numbers in problems
- Does not remember number words or digits
- Writes numbers illegibly
- Starts the calculation from the wrong place
- Cannot copy numbers accurately
- Exhibits left-right disorientation of numbers
- Omits digits on left or right side of a number
- Does not recognize operator signs (e.g., +, –)

Note. Adapted from "Characteristic Behaviors of Students With LD Who Have Teacher-Identified Math Weaknesses," by D. P. Bryant, B. Bryant, and D. D. Hammill, 2000, *Journal of Learning Disabilities, 33,* 168–177, 199. Copyright 2000 by PRO-ED, Inc. Reprinted with permission.

TABLE 2

Sample Division Curriculum Across the Grade Levels

- Model and solve simple problems involving division.
- Model, create, and describe division situations in which a set of concrete objects is separated into equivalent sets.
- Compute division facts with automaticity.
- Use repeated subtraction, equal sharing, and forming equal groups with remainders to do division.
- Use the inverse relationship of multiplication and division to compute and check results.
- Use models to solve division problems and use number sentences to record the solutions.
- Solve division problems in which a multidigit number is evenly divided by a one-digit number $(135 \div 5 = \underline{\quad})$.
- Understand the special properties of 0 and 1 in division (see Table 3).
- Demonstrate an understanding of, and the ability to use, standard algorithms for dividing a multidigit number by a one-digit number; use relationships between them to simplify computations and to check results.
- Use division to solve problems involving whole numbers (no more than two-digit divisors and three-digit dividends without technology).
- Demonstrate proficiency with division, including division with positive decimals and long division with multidigit divisors.
- Understand the concept of division of fractions.
- Compute and perform simple division of fractions and apply these procedures to solving problems.
- Solve problems involving division of positive fractions and explain why a particular operation was used for a given situation.
- Explain the meaning of division of positive fractions and perform the calculations.
- Solve division problems, including those arising in concrete situations that use positive and negative integers and combinations of these operations.
- Divide rational numbers (integers, fractions, and terminating decimals) and take positive rational numbers to whole-number powers.
- Interpret negative whole-number powers as repeated division or multiplication by the multiplicative inverse. Simplify and evaluate expressions that include exponents.
- Divide monomials; extend the process of taking powers and extracting roots to monomials when the latter results in a monomial with an integer exponent.
- Divide monomials and polynomials. Students solve multistep problems, including word problems, by using these techniques.
- Divide rational expressions and functions. Students solve both computationally and conceptually challenging problems by using these techniques.
- Divide complex numbers.
- Divide, reduce, and evaluate rational expressions with monomial and polynomial denominators and simplify complicated rational expressions, including those with negative exponents in the denominator.

the grade levels for division instruction and Table 3 provides division rules and relationships from the curriculum that must be taught.

The teaching of the division process is the focus of this article; space limitations restrict the content to the teaching of division basic facts and whole-number computation. First, we present an overview of division instruction. Then, we provide sample interventions for teaching division basic facts and whole-number computation. The interventions include explicit and strategic instructional procedures to teach students *how to do* division.

TABLE 3

Division Rules and Relationships

Rules
1. Zero divided by any number equals 0.
2. Any number divided by 1 equals the number.
3. Any number divided by the same number equals 1.

Relationships
1. Multiplication and division facts have the same numbers, just in different order.
$$7 \times 6 = 42$$
$$42 \div 6 = 7$$
$$42 \div 7 = 6$$
2. Because multiplication and division are related, you can always state a division problem as a multiplication problem.
$$56 \div 7 = ?$$
$$? \times 7 = 56$$
3. To check a division answer, multiply your answer by the number that the total is being divided by. If the answer to this multiplication problem equals the total, your answer is correct.
$$24 \div 8 = 3$$
$$3 \times 8 = 24$$

Source: S. P. Miller, S. Strawser, & C. D. Mercer (1996). Promoting strategic math performance among students with learning disabilities. *LD Forum*. Copyright 1996 by the Council for Learning Disabilities. Reprinted by permission.

OVERVIEW OF DIVISION INSTRUCTION

Division is a complex skill to teach because it requires prerequisite knowledge related to other mathematical skills. Drawing from cognitive and developmental psychology and behavioral theory, the knowledge base of what constitutes effective instructional practices for students with MLD has increased significantly in recent years (Miller, Butler, & Lee, 1998). Researchers (Carnine, 1997; Cawley & Parmar, 1992; Mercer & Miller, 1992; Rivera & Smith, 1987) have identified critical instructional and curricular variables that promote effective programming for students with MLD. Reviews of math intervention literature (Maccini & Hughes, 1997; Mastropieri, Scruggs, & Shiah, 1991; Miller et al., 1998) reveal that researchers have identified ways to teach division basic facts and whole-number computation at the elementary and secondary levels. For instance, Miller et al. (1998) concluded from their review that students with MLD benefit from strategy and self-regulation instruction that uses step-by-step processes for guiding thinking, and that manipulatives can promote mathematical performance in computation. Miller et al. (1998) noted that across interventions, modeling, guided practice, and independent practice were common instructional procedures. Additionally, the stages-of-learning model (Rivera & Smith, 1997) has been helpful in guiding the selection of interventions and the delivery of instruction. This knowledge base is important because as students engage in increasingly complex mathematical curricula, they must be able to draw upon basic knowledge and skills to help them solve higher order thinking mathematical problems.

Stages of Learning

In the stages of learning model, five stages of learning are identified: acquisition, proficiency, maintenance, generalization, and adaptation (problem solving). Taking division as an example, when introduced to a new division skill, the *acquisition* stage of learning is characterized by a student having little or no understanding or accuracy in performing the skill. After a period of instruction, students should demonstrate accurate performance. Depending on the skill, students must also be able to perform the skill accurately and quickly to reach automaticity (i.e., practicing skills until they require less cognitive processing), which is considered the *proficiency* stage of learning. Students need to be able to perform certain division skills (e.g., computing basic facts) proficiently so that they can perform commensurate with their peers and complete work in the designated class period. For example, if students can correctly compute basic division facts but do so too slowly, they will probably have difficulty with whole-number computation and other more advanced division skills; thus, allocating time to practice fact-fluency building should be part of a mathematics program (Cooke & Reichard, 1996; Salisbury, 1990). Hasselbring, Goin, and Bransford (1988) noted that the development of automaticity is important to success with higher level skills. Students should be able to perform lower order or "tool" skills automatically so that more emphasis can be placed on higher order skills. The *maintenance* stage of learning focuses on students remembering how to perform skills at mastery levels. Thus, periodic evaluation for retention is necessary to ensure that students are retaining the knowledge and skills necessary for more complex skill instruction. During the *generalization* stage of learning, the learned skill should transfer to other situations, settings, and so forth. For some students with MLD, skills learned in the classroom do not appear to be automatically generalized without further instruction. It is recommended that generalization be introduced to students during the acquisition stage of learning and specifically programmed following demonstration of skill mastery (Deshler & Schumaker, 1986; Ellis, Lenz, & Sabornie, 1987). The last stage of learning is often referred to as *adaptation or problem solving*. Until recently, problem solving was a neglected skill in mathematical instruction. Fortunately, the National Council of Teachers of Mathematics (NCTM, 2000) standards stress the importance of integrating problem-solving situations into math instruction when introducing skills and concepts.

Explicit and Strategic Instruction

A meta-analysis on academic treatment outcomes, including mathematics, for students with LD identified the positive contribution (i.e., higher effect sizes) of explicit and strategic instructional procedures compared to other instructional approaches (Swanson, Hoskyn, & Lee, 1999). Findings from this meta-analysis distinguished differences and overlapping similarities between explicit and strategic instructional procedures.

Differences in the instructional procedures center on the focus of the approach (Swanson, 2001). Explicit instruction focuses on the teaching of subskills (e.g., division facts, multidigit dividend divided by a 1-digit divisor with no remainder) that are identified as in need of instruction. These subskills are sequenced and taught to students usually in small group instruction. Instructional procedures include a "perky pace," multiple opportunities for students to practice and respond, feedback, and progress monitoring. Strategic instruction focuses on rules and the process of learning including metacognitive (e.g., self-regulatory) cues and the use of mnemonics for memory retention and retrieval (Swanson, 2001). Strategic instructional procedures include a rationale for learning the strategy and specific steps to activate cognitive and meta-cognitive processes.

Swanson et al. (1999) found that students benefit from a combined model (CM) of direct (or explicit) and strategic instruction that consists of an overlap or similarity of instructional procedures. The similarities shared by the two approaches include sequencing of instruction, providing instructional routines that consist of a sequence of events (e.g., presentation of subject matter, guided practice, and independent practice), focusing on mass practice, overlearning, teaching to criterion, and evaluating student learning on a regular basis (Swanson, 2001). Also, small group instruction is a procedure that is shared by both instructional approaches. Small group instruction is an effective way to provide explicit and strategic instruction and to address the wide range of math abilities found in any classroom. In small groups, students are given more opportunities to express what they know and receive immediate feedback from the teacher and other students (Vaughn, Moody, & Schumm, 1998).

Additionally, Swanson et al. (1999) found that the specific instructional components that are common to the CM "increase the predictive power of treatment effectiveness beyond what can be predicted by variations in methodology and age" (p. 218). The instructional components that comprise the combined model are presented in Table 4. Based on these findings of treatment effects, division instruction for students with MLD should include a combined instructional approach using explicit and strategic instruction as appropriate.

SAMPLE INTERVENTIONS TO TEACH DIVISION

The following interventions can be used to teach division basic facts and whole-number computation. Table 5 links the instructional procedures used in each intervention to the practices from the CM of instruction identified in the Swanson et al. (1999) meta-analysis of treatment outcomes.

Concrete-Semiconcrete-Abstract (CSA) (Miller & Mercer, 1993)

Recognizing the abstract nature of symbolic-based mathematical instruction, the concrete-semiconcrete-abstract (CSA) teaching sequence is an example of how instruction can be

TABLE 4

Instructional Components in the Combined Model

- Sequencing: breaking down of the task, fading of prompts or cues, sequencing short activities, giving step-by-step prompts.
- Drill-repetition and practice-review: daily testing of skills, for example, statements in the treatment description related to mastery criteria, distributed review and practice, using redundant materials or text, repeated practice, sequenced review, daily feedback, and/or weekly reviews.
- Segmentation: breaking down a targeted skill into smaller units and then synthesizing the parts into a whole.
- Directed questioning and responses: the teacher asks "process-related" and/or "content-related" questions of students.
- Control difficulty or processing demands of a task: tasks are sequenced from easy to difficult and only necessary hints and probes are provided to the child.
- Technology: for example, use of a computer.
- Modeling of problem-solving steps by teacher: teacher provides a demonstration of processes or steps to solve problems or explains how to do a task.
- Group instruction: instruction occurs in a small group; students and/or teacher interact within the group.
- A supplement to teacher or peer involvement: may include homework, or a parent or someone else who assists instruction.
- Strategy cues: reminders to use strategies or multisteps; for example, the teacher verbalizes problem solving or procedures to solve, instruction makes use of "think-aloud" models, teacher presents benefits of strategy use or procedures.

Note. Adapted from *Interventions for students with learning disabilities. A meta-analysis of treatment outcomes*, by H. L. Swanson, M. Hoskyn, & C. Lee (1999) NY: Guilford. Adapted by permission.

TABLE 5
Linkages Between the Interventions and the Combined Model Instructional Components

	Instructional Components[a]									
Intervention	*1*	*2*	*3*	*4*	*5*	*6*	*7*	*8*	*9*	*10*
Concrete-Semiconcrete-Abstract	✓	✓		✓			✓	✓		✓
Interspersal Drill Ratios	✓	✓							✓	
Number Families	✓	✓	✓				✓	✓		✓
DRAW and SOLVE		✓		✓			✓	✓		✓
Pacing	✓	✓	✓							
Benchmark		✓		✓						
Demonstration + Permanent Model	✓	✓					✓	✓		✓
Key Questions	✓	✓	✓	✓			✓			✓
Alternative Algorithms	✓	✓	✓				✓	✓		✓

[a]See Table 4 for a description of the Instructional Components.

delivered to promote understanding and mastery. The CSA teaching sequence was examined as a way to teach place value (Peterson, Mercer, & O'Shea, 1988) and basic facts (Miller & Mercer, 1993; Miller, Mercer, & Dillon, 1992). In both studies, skill instruction was presented initially by providing representation of a number concept via manipulatives (e.g., popsicle sticks, buttons). After several lessons, the representation changed to semiconcrete involving tally marks instead of manipulatives for an additional number of lessons. Finally, students received abstract representation only by solving simple equations. Results indicated that students learned the skills to criterion suggesting that for some students with MLD the CSA teaching procedure is highly effective.

The CSA teaching procedures begin with the teacher providing an advance organizer about the purpose of the lesson. Next, in the demonstration procedure, the teacher models how to solve the problem while verbalizing the steps ("thinking aloud"). The teacher asks questions, "What is the first thing that I do?" Once the demonstration is completed, a guided practice procedure is implemented. Students work on several problems and the teacher provides prompts and cues as necessary. A prompt might include, "You have the correct number of sticks for the first number, now which number do you look at?" Corrective feedback and assistance are provided immediately. Finally, students work independently to complete 10 problems. To solve problems during guided practice, in the concrete phase students use manipulatives, in the semiconcrete phase tallies are used, and in the abstract phase, students are instructed to solve the problem using numerals only. A criterion of 80% correct is required during independent practice.

Interspersal Drill Ratios (Cooke & Reichard, 1996)

This intervention involves sets of flashcards that contain a predetermined ratio of known and unknown facts. The unknown facts are interspersed among the known facts for practice purposes. From Cooke and Reichard's (1996) study, results showed on the mastery and generalization tests that the majority of students did better when 70% of the facts were unknown (acquisition stage) and 30% were known (maintenance stage). These results suggest that instruction can be structured so students are not only learning a relatively large percentage of new facts but also are reviewing previously learned facts.

Interspersal drill ratios involves several components. First, through assessment procedures, teachers identify which division facts each student knows automatically (e.g., says the correct answer within 2 sec) and which facts are unknown automatically. The two groups of facts are written on flashcards and separated into two piles. Second, student pairs are identified to work together in a peer-tutoring format. The format consists of the following procedures: the tutor and student work together; the tutor shows the student a flashcard with a problem and says the problem; the tutor waits for no more than 2 sec for a response; depending on the response, the tutor gives corrective feedback or praise; the cards are shuffled and another round is presented. The roles are reversed. Third, at the end of the tutoring session, a mastery test is given. The mastery test consists of each flashcard shown to the student for up to 2 sec. If the response is correct, then the card is placed in the pocket with a " + "; cards with incorrect responses are placed in the " − " pocket. Finally, a generalization test is administered, which contains a worksheet of the first 15 facts taught.

Number Families (Bley & Thornton, 1995)

Instruction in number families involves learning the relationship between multiplication and division facts to solve problems. Using number families, students learn division facts with a one-digit dividend and one-digit divisor and are taught the corresponding multiplication facts. For example, given 6 ÷ 2 is 3, students are taught that 6 ÷ 3 is 2, 3 × 2 = 6, and 2 × 3 = 6, all within the same lesson. Teachers model the process for students using manipulatives while "thinking aloud" how they solve the problems and the relationship among the facts. Student progress can be determined through flashcard presentation of the facts with a 2-sec response time or by having students complete a 1-min timing on a probe, which contains all facts taught to determine if students generalize their learning from the flashcards to the fluency-building probe.

DRAW (Miller & Mercer, 1991) and SOLVE (Miller & Mercer, 1993)

The DRAW strategy includes a mnemonic that can be used to promote the acquisition of basic facts. The steps include D = Discover the sign, R = Read the problem, A = Answer or draw and check, and W = Write the answer. The DRAW strategy includes a semiconcrete component (i.e., draw) if needed by students to answer the fact. The SOLVE strategy includes a mnemonic that is intended to facilitate memory. The steps of the mnemonic are S = See the sign, O = Observe and answer (if unable to answer, keep going), L = Look and draw, V = Verify your answer, and E = enter your answer. The instructional steps include (a) provide an advance organizer explaining the purpose of the lesson; (b) model and "think aloud" how to use the mnemonic to solve problems; and (c) teach students the mnemonic (say the mnemonic, name the letters, tell what to do for each letter). Students should learn the steps of the strategies to mastery and then use the strategies to compute problems.

Pacing (Rivera, 1996; Ryberg & Sebastian, 1983)

The Pacing strategy can be used with students who are ready to move from the acquisition to proficiency stage of learning with division facts. This fluency-building strategy involves the use of devices (e.g., prerecorded audiotapes, and metronomes) with an audible signal and adjustable intervals (e.g., 25 beeps/min, 40 beeps/min). The interval can be set at increasingly faster rates until students attain the desired criterion rate for mastery. Given a worksheet with the targeted problems, the students are instructed to work from left to right, to write an answer on their worksheet each time they hear the beep, and to skip problems they do not know when the sound occurs. Skipped problems become "learning opportunities" rather than errors, and can be taught through error-drill procedures, including peer tutoring, interspersal drill ratio, and number families.

Benchmark (Rivera & Smith, 1997)

The Benchmark strategy is an effective fluency-building technique. Given a worksheet of facts and working in a left-to-right progression, a fact (Benchmark) is designated as the target to reach by the end of the 1-min timing. The designated fact can be starred, circled, or identified in any manner by students. Rewards can be distributed for students who reach their Benchmark. The Benchmark fact is determined by (a) identifying the number of correct problems previously answered in a 1-min timing, (b) multiplying that number by 10%, and (c) adding the 10% figure to the original figure; this new number becomes the Benchmark for the next 1-min timing. For example, if a student computed 20 problems correct in 1 min on Monday, then the Benchmark figure is 22. The Benchmark strategy promotes self-competition ("beat yesterday's score") and can be motivating for some students.

Demonstration Plus Permanent Model (Smith & Lovitt, 1975; Rivera & Smith, 1987, 1988)

The Demonstration Plus Permanent Model (D+PM) technique is useful for the acquisition stage of learning and can be used to teach whole-number computation including long division. There are several steps involved in this teaching technique. First, the teacher selects problems from student work that warrant explicit instruction (i.e., acquisition stage of learning). Second, the teacher works with a small group of students to teach them the process by demonstrating how to perform the algorithm and thinking aloud the steps, by having students imitate the process on similar problems, and by leaving a completed model as a referent on the student's worksheet in case a permanent model is needed for cueing purposes. Rivera and Smith (1988) found that D+PM worked well and quickly to teach students whole-number computation to mastery (90% accuracy for 3 days).

Key Questions (Rivera & Smith, 1988)

When solving long division, some students can become confused while solving multi-step division problems. Rivera and Smith (1988) found that the D+PM strategy worked well when paired with key questions. The strategy paired with key questions can help students get back on track if they are confused by where they are in the division process. The questions include

(1) What is the problem?
(2) What are the steps?
(3) What did you just do?
(4) What do you do next?

Through modeling and "thinking aloud," students are taught to ask themselves these questions or to refer to a chart or cue card with the questions, thus promoting more self-directed learning.

Alternative Algorithms

An algorithm is a routine, step-by-step procedure used in computation. Examples of alternative algorithms include Partial Products and Expanded Notation. Partial Products is a technique that can be used to teach division (McCoy & Prehm, 1987). This technique helps students focus on place value and the quantity that is actually partitioned (see the following).

Partial Products (McCoy & Prehm, 1987)

$$428 \div 2 = ?$$

$400 \div 2 = 200$	200
$20 \div 2 = 10$	10
$8 \div 2 = 4$	+4
	$\overline{214}$

Expanded Notation (Cawley & Parmar, 1992)

Expanded Notation can be used as an alternative algorithm to typical instructional algorithms for whole-number division computation. The Expanded Notation algorithm enables students to show place value representations of numerals and to calculate answers (see the following).

$$428 \div 2 = ?$$
$$(400 + 20 + 8) \div 2 =$$
$$(200 + 10 + 4) = 214$$

For both types of alternative algorithms, teachers model and "think aloud" how they solve a division problem. Students imitate and verbalize the steps in using these algorithms, use manipulatives to represent the process, or work with a partner to solve problems.

Sequence of Instruction (Rivera & Smith, 1987; Rivera & Smith, 1988)

Teachers usually present information to students in a task analyzed, sequenced format. Students are taught the easiest skill in the sequence first. Once that skill is mastered, the next one is presented, and so on. Investigations have revealed that students do not have to be taught whole-number computational skills in an easy-to-difficult sequence for learning to occur. Rather, the most difficult skill within a group can be taught because, in general, students tend to generalize the process to easier problems. Manipulatives can be used to promote place value understanding.

The following guidelines are offered:

(1) Develop a task analysis of whole-number computation (e.g., 2-digit dividend divided by 1-digit divisor, 3-digit dividend divided by 1-digit divisor, 3-digit dividend divided by 2-digit divisor).

(2) Test students to determine which skills within the sequence are mastered and which skills require instruction.

(3) Select the most difficult skill within a group as the instructional target (e.g., 3-digit dividend divided by 2-digit divisor).

(4) Teach the most difficult skill using the D+ PM strategy and Key Questions strategy (for example).

(5) Present problems on a worksheet representing all of the skills within a group (e.g., 2-digit dividend divided by 1-digit divisor, 3-digit dividend divided by 1-digit divisor, 3-digit dividend divided by 2-digit divisor).

(6) Collect student performance data on all of the skills on the work sheet.

CONCLUSIONS

Research indicates that students with MLD perform consistently below their peers at the elementary and secondary level on basic mathematical skills (Cawley & Miller, 1989). Skill deficits can impede students' ability to comprehend and master a variety of mathematical concepts. Division is a complex skill that is part of the curriculum across the grades; yet division instruction may not receive the attention it deserves. Consequently, when students are asked to solve higher order mathematical problems, they may lack the division knowledge and skills that are necessary to solve problems. Research has indicated that students with MLD respond favorably to instruction in academics, including mathematics, when explicit and strategic instructional procedures are employed. The purpose of this paper was to provide an overview of division instruction and sample interventions that feature the combined model of instructional components (i.e., explicit and strategic instructional procedures) for teaching division. Our focus was on teaching students *how to do* division. By using effective instructional procedures, students can master division skills when instruction is provided systematically and regularly as part of daily mathematics teaching.

REFERENCES

Bley, N. S., & Thornton, C. A. (1995). *Teaching mathematics to students with learning disabilities*. Austin, TX: PRO-ED.

Bryant, D. P., Bryant, B., & Hammill, D. (2000). Characteristic behaviors of students with LD who have teacher-identified math weaknesses. *Journal of Learning Disabilities, 33,* 168–177.

Carnine, D. (1997). Instructional design in mathematics for students with learning disabilities. *Journal of Learning Disabilities, 30*(2), 130–141.

Cawley, J. F., & Foley, T. E. (2003). About the mathematics of division: Implications for students with disabilities. *Exceptionality, 11,* 131–149.

Cawley, J. F., & Miller, J. H. (1989). Cross-sectional comparisons of the mathematical performance of children with learning disabilities: Are we on the right track toward comprehensive programming? *Journal of Learning Disabilities, 23,* 250–254, 259.

Cawley, J. F., & Parmar, R. S. (1992). Arithmetic programming for students with disabilities: An alternative. *Remedial and Special Education, 13*(3), 6–18.

Cooke, N. L., & Reichard, S. M. (1996). The effects of different interspersal drill ratios on acquisition and generalization of multiplication and division facts. *Education and Treatment of Children, 19*(2), 124–142.

Deshler, D. D., & Schumaker, J. B. (1986). Learning strategies: An instructional alternative for low-achieving adolescents. *Exceptional Children, 52,* 583–590.

Ellis, E. S., Lenz, B. K., & Sabornie, E. J. (1987). Generalization and adaptation of learning strategies to natural environments: Part I-critical agents. *Remedial and Special Education, 8*(1), 6–21.

Garnett, K., & Fleischner, J. (1983). Automatization and basic fact performance of normal and learning disabled children. *Learning Disability Quarterly, 6,* 223–230.

Geary, D. C. (1990). A componential analysis of an early learning deficit in mathematics. *Journal of Experimental Child Psychology, 49,* 363–383.

Geary, D. C. (in press). Mathematics and learning disabilities. *Journal of Learning Disabilities.*

Hasselbring, T. S., Goin, L. I., & Bransford, J. D. (1988). Developing math automaticity in learning handicapped children: The role of computerized drill and practice. *Focus on Exceptional Children, 20*(6), 1–7.

Jordan, N. C., Levine, S. C., & Huttenlocher, J. (1995). Calculation abilities of young children with different patterns of cognitive functioning. *Journal of Learning Disabilities, 28,* 53–64.

Maccini, P., & Hughes, C. A. (1997). Mathematics interventions for adolescents with learning disabilities. *Learning Disabilities Research & Practice, 12,* 168–176.

Mastropieri, M. A., Scruggs, T. E., & Shiah, S. (1991). Mathematics instruction for learning disabled students: A review of research. *Learning Disabilities Research & Practice, 6,* 89–98.

McCoy, E. M., & Prehm, H. J. (1987). *Teaching mainstreamed students. Methods and techniques.* Denver, CO: Love Publishing Company.

Mercer, C. D., & Miller, S. P. (1992). Teaching students with learning problems in math to acquire, understand, and apply basic math facts. *Remedial and Special Education, 13*(3), 19–35, 61.

Miller, S. P., Butler, F. M., & Lee, K. (1998). Validated practices for teaching mathematics to students with learning disabilities: A review of literature. *Focus on Exceptional Children, 31*(1), 1–24.

Miller, S. P., & Mercer, C. D. (1991). *Addition facts 0 to 9.* Lawrence, KS: Edge Enterprises.

Miller, S. P., & Mercer, C. D. (1993). Using data to learn about concrete-semiconcrete-abstract instruction for students with math disabilities. *Learning Disabilities Research & Practice, 8,* 89–96.

Miller, S. P., Mercer, C. D., & Dillon, A. (1992). CSA: Acquiring and retaining math skills. *Intervention in School and Clinic, 28,* 105–110.

Miller, S. P., Strawser, S., & Mercer, C. D. (1996). Promoting strategic math performance among students with learning disabilities. *LD Forum, 21*(2), 34–40.

National Council of Teachers of Mathematics. (2000). *Principles and standards for school mathematics.* Reston, VA: Author.

Peterson, S., Mercer, C. D., & O'Shea, L. (1988). Teaching learning disabled students place value using the concrete to abstract sequence. *Learning Disabilities Research, 4,* 52–56.

Rivera, D. M., & Smith, D. D. (1987). Influence of modeling on acquisition and generalization of computational skills: A summary of research findings from three sites. *Learning Disability Quarterly, 10,* 69–80.

Rivera, D. M., & Smith, D. D. (1988). Using a demonstration strategy to teach midschool students with learning disabilities how to compute long division. *Journal of Learning Disabilities, 21,* 77–81.

Rivera, D. M., & Smith, D. D. (1997). *Teaching students with learning and behavior problems* (3rd ed.). Boston: Allyn & Bacon.

Rivera, D. P. (1996). Using cooperative learning to teach mathematics to students with learning disabilities. *LD Forum, 21*(3), 29–33.

Ryberg, S., & Sebastian, J. (1983, April). *What to do if your chart goes flat: Pacing.* Paper presented at the International Conference of the Council for Exceptional Children, Detroit, MI.

Salisbury, D. F. (1990). Cognitive psychology and its implications for designing drill and practice for programs for computers. *Journal of Computer Based Instruction, 17*(1), 23–30.

Smith, D. D., & Lovitt, T. C. (1975). The use of modeling techniques to influence the acquisition of computational arithmetic skills in learning-disabled children. In E. Ramp & G. Semb (Eds.), *Behavior analysis: Areas of research and application*. Englewood Cliffs, NJ: Prentice Hall.

Swanson, H. L. (2001). Reading intervention research outcomes and students with learning disabilities: What are the major instructional ingredients for successful outcomes? *Perspectives, 27*(2), 18–20.

Swanson, H. L., Hoskyn, M., & Lee, C. (1999). *Interventions for students with learning disabilities. A meta-analysis of treatment outcomes*. New York: Guilford Press.

Vaughn, S., Moody, S. W., & Schumm, J. S. (1998). Broken promises: Reading instruction in the resource room. *Exceptional Children, 64*, 211–225.

Teaching Division to Students With Learning Disabilities: A Constructivist Approach

Marjorie Montague

Special Education Department
University of Miami

This article focuses on understanding the teaching and learning of Division from a constructivist perspective. An overview of constructivism is provided first to set the stage for understanding the rationale underlying the move toward the use of a constructivist approach for teaching mathematics. In this special issue, the emphasis is on teaching and learning Division, but the principles discussed can be applied generally across topics within the domain of mathematics. Conceptual and procedural understanding of Division is discussed in the context of both computation and word problem solving. Suggestions are given for teaching students with learning disabilities, using a constructivist framework.

Mathematics has been at the forefront of the school reform movement for over a decade. The publication of the *Curriculum and Evaluation Standards for School Mathematics* (National Council of Teachers of Mathematics, NCTM, 1989) and the subsequent revision, the *Principles and Standards for School Mathematics* (NCTM, 2000), provided direction for both pedagogical and curricular reforms. Changes have occurred nationwide in the mathematics curriculum and the content of instruction, teaching methodology and practice, learning tasks and activities, the context and structure for learning, and assessment and evaluation. The following six principles have guided educators in their move toward reform in mathematics education (Woodward & Montague, 2002):

1. equal opportunity in mathematics for all students,
2. a comprehensive and coordinated curriculum across grades,
3. excellent teachers who have the content and pedagogical knowledge for assessing and instructing students,
4. active construction of knowledge by students who are empowered mathematically,
5. appropriate assessment that provides direction for instruction and supports learning, and
6. technology as an essential component of mathematics teaching and learning.

Requests for reprints should be sent to Marjorie Montague, Special Education Department, University of Miami, P.O. Box 248065, Coral Gables, FL 33124. E-mail: mmontague@miami.edu

Teaching practices advocated by the NCTM *Standards* include providing extensive experience for students with meaningful activities as the foundation for conceptual understanding, a variety of hands-on materials to promote physical and mental mathematical representations at both the concrete and abstract levels, a problem-solving context that encourages and supports discussion and communication among students about mathematics, and constant opportunities for children to build on their mathematical knowledge and develop new ideas. The NCTM *Standards* reflect a cognitive and constructivist approach to teaching and learning mathematics, which is a dramatic departure from the rote-learning model that had dominated mathematics instruction until the late 1980s.

The constructivist approach underscores the social–interactive nature of learning and views children as active and engaged learners who construct meaning by selecting, organizing, connecting, and understanding information, ideas, and concepts as a consequence of prior knowledge and experience. In mathematics reform classrooms, the emphasis is on student discourse and debate of mathematical concepts. Teachers probe and question carefully but persistently, as students acquire a greater conceptual understanding. Through dialogue, teachers introduce mathematical vocabulary, clarify concepts, and refine students' thinking. Students become accustomed to verbalizing their ideas and asking thoughtful, provocative questions. Ensuring that all students are actively engaged can be a formidable task, however, given the wide variability of student ability, achievement, and motivation in a typical classroom. At the same time, more and more students with disabilities are receiving their mathematics education in general education classrooms.

Barriers to full implementation of the NCTM *Standards* have to do not only with individual student differences, but also with teacher beliefs and behavior. Maccini and Gagnon (2002) surveyed 129 secondary general and special education mathematics teachers about the *Standards*. The majority of teachers indicated that they had not heard of the *Standards*, and also reported that they taught mostly basic skills or general mathematics in a traditional manner to students with learning disabilities (LD). Baxter, Woodward, Voorhies, and Wong (2002) found that the greatest challenge for the teachers in their study of mathematics reform classrooms was how to include all students, including low achievers and those with cognitive and behavioral disabilities, in classroom discussions. These students display a variety of characteristics that can impede their participation in classroom activities and adversely affect their mathematical performance (Montague, 1996).

LD may be manifested in memory and strategic deficits, which can cause difficulty in conceptualizing mathematical operations, representing and recalling mathematical facts, conceptualizing and learning algorithms and formulae, and solving mathematical problems. Problems with language and communication may prevent full participation in discussions and debate about mathematical ideas and concepts. Understanding problem situations and how to represent them mathematically seems to be a common difficulty for these students (Montague & Applegate, 2001). Also, noncognitive factors such as low motivation, poor self-esteem, and repeated failure can undermine a student's confidence and desire to become an empowered learner. Thus, there is a myriad of cognitive and noncognitive attributes that prevent a child from succeeding in mathematics, generally, and in mathematical problem solving, specifically. Understanding the idio-syncratic learning characteristics and behaviors of these children will help teachers adapt and adjust instruction, so that all students will profit from participation in reform-based, constructivist classrooms.

The following sections focus on strategies to enhance mathematics teaching and learning for students with LD. In keeping with the theme of this special issue, Division is the topic of discussion.

DIVISION AND COMPUTATION

Mathematics educators have seriously begun to question whether we should continue to teach the long Division algorithm (Bley & Thornton, 1995). Their reasoning is that long Division is rarely used in daily life and, if it is needed, using a calculator to com-pute produces a faster and more accurate solution. If students understand the concep-tual underpinnings of Division, there seems to be no rationale for requiring students to practice the algorithm for weeks at a time. Geary (1994) makes the point that com-pared with the other three mathematical operations, little research has been done on the psychological processes used in obtaining solutions to Division problems. Stu-dents with LD are particularly vulnerable because they often experience visual pro-cessing difficulties that can thwart even the best effort to complete a Division algo-rithm with a two- or three-digit divisor. Their ability to perform the necessary operations sequentially and speedily makes Division an aversive activity for most of these students.

A constructivist approach to teaching Division would use problem situations such as the following to engender "sense-making" in students and develop conceptual under-standing of the process of Division. Here are three typical Division computations and corresponding word problems appropriate for primary, intermediate, and upper-level students:

Primary Level
2/6   Solution:

$$2\overline{)6}^{\;3}$$

José has 6 pieces of candy. He wants to give half of the candies to his friend, Andy. How many pieces of candy will each boy get?
Intermediate Level
3/1503   Solution:

$$3\overline{)1503}^{\;\;501}$$
$$\underline{15}$$
$$03$$
$$\underline{03}$$

Three airplane tickets cost $1,503. How much does one ticket cost?
Upper Level
12/276   Solution:

$$
\begin{array}{r}
23 \\
12\overline{)276} \\
\underline{24} \\
36 \\
\underline{36}
\end{array}
$$

The class is having a play in the school gym. There are 276 chairs. The teacher wants the children to arrange the chairs in rows with 12 chairs in each row. How many rows will there be?

Similar to the other arithmetic operations, Division seems to have the same regularities (Geary, 1994). That is, children tend to use preexisting knowledge or related concepts when learning a new concept, and their problem-solving errors tend to be systematic. When first presented with Division problems, children tend to rely on their knowledge of multiplication and/or addition. Recall of multiplication facts such as $2 \times 3 = 6$ to solve the primary problem or successive multiplication such as $3 \times 2 = 6$, $3 \times 3 = 9$, $3 \times 4 = 12$, and, finally, $3 \times 5 = 15$ for a partial solution to the intermediate problem are typical multiplication references. Repeated additions or subtractions are other strategies frequently used by children who are learning Division. For example, to solve 2/6, primary-level children might simply add $2 + 2 + 2 = 6$ and then count the number of twos they added (three).

Division becomes even more complicated when the dividend is not evenly divided by the divisor. The concept of remainders in Division is introduced first in primary school with whole number division and then, later in elementary school, when remainders are expressed in fractions and decimals. Although most children will learn the rote procedures for computing Division problems with remainders, they likely will experience difficulties if these same computations are introduced within situational contexts such as the following example provided by Silver (1992, p. 29): "Mary has 100 brownies which she will put into containers that hold exactly 40 brownies each. (a) How many containers will she fill?, (b) How many containers will she use for all the brownies?, (c) After she fills as many containers as she can, how many brownies will be left over?"

Interestingly, even though most children will have a basic understanding that Division involves determining the number of subsets of a smaller number contained in the larger number, their performance declines dramatically when the same problems are presented in the context of simple word problems such as those mentioned earlier (Geary, 1994). Montague and Applegate (2001) found that perception of the difficulty level of word problems by students with LD influenced their persistence in solving problems. In fact, a simple one-step Division problem was perceived to be as difficult as a more complex two-step problem, requiring multiplication and subtraction. Unlike their average-achieving and academically gifted peers, these students tended to give up without much of an attempt.

Constructivists would advocate bypassing algorithmic instruction in favor of presenting problem situations for students to discuss and solve in small groups. These problem-solving groups would be provided first with physical materials to facilitate representation and eventually progress to more abstract symbolic representations. Within the problem-solving context, a variety of algorithms would be introduced based on the students' solutions to the problems. There seems to be a growing consensus that alternative algorithms should be taught to students, particularly those who have difficulty with traditional approaches (Bley & Thornton, 1995; Foley & Cawley, this issue; Woodward & Montague, 2002). Learning alternative algorithms helps children develop conceptual understanding and articulate the reasoning they use to arrive at solutions to Division problems. Faulty reasoning and misconceptions are more easily detected and understood within a problem-solving context.

Some students seem to understand the concept of Division but still have difficulty with algorithmic procedures. Procedural difficulty may have to do with memory deficits, fact-retrieval problems, an inability to sequence and switch operations, or perseveration problems. Bley and Thornton (1995) suggested a sequence of activities for teaching long Division to these students. Manipulatives (e.g., chips), prompts (e.g., red stoplight above the last skip counting box), and cues (e.g., a card listing the sequence of operations) should be provided initially and faded as appropriate. Students progress through the sequence of activities until they are able to perform problems with a four-digit dividend and a two-digit divisor. Cawley, Fitzmaurice-Hayes, and Shaw (1988) developed a similar sequence of activities for acquisition of procedural knowledge in Division.

Calculators to facilitate computation should be introduced for students with LD in primary school. It is important to select the most appropriate type for each student and teach him or her how to use them for accurate and efficient computation (Bley & Thornton, 1995). Computers with printouts, for example, are helpful for students who need to check if they entered the numbers accurately. For students with visual processing problems, large print or color printouts may be helpful, whereas talking calculators may help students with auditory processing problems. Calculators that allow input that reflects typical linear sequences are best for most students. They can be integrated into paper-and-pencil activities when students are learning Division algorithms and eventually replace paper-and-pencil computation altogether.

DIVISION AND PROBLEM SOLVING

Solving mathematical word problems is a complex activity requiring a variety of cognitive processes necessary for representing problems and executing solutions. A primary difference between good and poor problem solvers is the ability to represent problems (e.g., Montague & Applegate, 2001). Problem representation requires the problem solver to translate linguistic and numerical information into a coherent, integrated problem structure or description. The problem solver must then use this verbal, graphic, symbolic, and/or quantitative representation to generate appropriate mathematical equations and operations and solve the problem (Montague, 2002).

Good problem solvers understand the semantic elements of problems as well as the mathematical or numerical properties. Two cognitive processes that facilitate this understanding are paraphrasing and visualizing. Paraphrasing, a good reading comprehension strategy, involves translating the linguistic information by rephrasing or restating the problem without altering the meaning of the problem. Students can be taught to "put the problem into their own words." Students can convert the problem into their own story and tell the story to others. In this way, they become facile in conveying the meaning of the problem to others and to themselves. Visualization is a cognitive process that helps students form internal representations of the problem in memory. They can be taught to use three-dimensional manipulatives to represent the problem, draw a representation on paper, or make a mental image of the problem. It is insufficient, however, to simply draw a picture of the problem. Students must be taught how to visually represent the relationships among the problem parts; that is, they must be taught how to develop schematic or relational images (Jitendra, DiPipi, & Perron-Jones, 2002).

Students with LD are characteristically poor mathematical problem solvers and, as such, most likely will have difficulty in a constructivist context that emphasizes individual construction of knowledge, conceptual understanding, and articulation of ideas and reasoning. However, with supplemental, intensive, and explicit instruction, students with LD may be able to participate more fully in inclusive mathematics classrooms. Additionally, it is essential that teachers have an understanding of the semantic and mathematical demands of the problems, the cognitive and metacognitive processes and strategies that facilitate problem solving, and the instructional principles that foster learning. We now return to the whole number Division problems mentioned earlier.

1. José has 6 pieces of candy. He wants to give half of the candies to his friend, Andy. How many pieces of candy will each boy get? (Primary level)
2. Three airplane tickets cost $1,503. How much does one ticket cost? (Intermediate level)
3. The class is having a play in the school gym. There are 276 chairs. The teacher wants the children to arrange the chairs in rows with 12 chairs in each row. How many rows will there be? (Upper level)

These problems have very different demands from the situation-specific Division problems with remainders studied by Silver (1992, p. 29):

4. Mary has 100 brownies, which she will put into containers that hold exactly 40 brownies each. (a) How many containers will she fill? (b) How many containers will she use for all the brownies? (c) After she fills as many containers as she can, how many brownies will be left over?

Semantic and Mathematical Demands

Teachers must have content knowledge of Division and be able to distinguish among the various types of Division problems. Division problems may be either measurement or partition problems (Burton, 1992; Foley & Cawley, this issue). Measurement problems (e.g., Problem 3) require the problem solver to make as many groups of the required size as possible. Partition problems (e.g., Problem 2) require understanding the numbers of sets needed and then dealing out the total number of objects into the sets. Problem 1 could be conceptualized either as a measurement or as a partition problem. Primary level students, particularly when given realistic manipulatives that actually represent the problem, have been found to be able to distinguish between these problem types, although partition problems seem to present more of a challenge for them (Burton, 1992). After grade 5, students do not seem to have difficulty with either type of problem. Furthermore, to solve Problem 1, students need to have a conceptual understanding of "half." Additionally, students must be able to understand the semantics of the problem and organize the linguistic information. Problem 2, for example, includes the number words, three and one. Problem 3 includes the word "arrange." These problems may be misunderstood by students with language processing difficulties.

When Division problems have remainders, the difficulty level increases. For the situation-specific problem presented above, the computation is constant across the problems (i.e., a, b, and c), but the answers are different (Silver, 1992). To solve Problem 4a, a quotient-only problem, students must ignore the remainder. To solve Problem 4b, an augmented-quotient problem, students must round up the answer to the nearest whole number. To solve Problem 4c, a remainder-only problem, students must ignore the quotient because the answer is the remainder only. Understanding the semantic subtleties of these types of Division problems can be frustrating for even good problem solvers and near to impossible for students with LD.

Cognitive and Metacognitive Processes and Strategies

A well-developed repertoire of cognitive and metacognitive processes and strategies allows students to engage in "sense-making" (Li & Silver, 2000). Students make sense of problems by understanding the problem conditions and goals, by executing strategies and procedures, and by interpreting their solutions and answers. In other words, the execution of a solution is directly tied to the problem solver's comprehension of the problem and their integration of the problem information. Academically low-achieving and underachieving students either do not have the necessary processes and strategies or do not utilize those they do have when solving problems. Therefore, it is essential to teach students these important processes and strategies that will help them become more effective and efficient problem solvers. With these tools, students should be more able to contribute and participate successfully in constructivist mathematics classes.

Students can be taught a problem-solving routine that incorporates the following essential cognitive processes for mathematical problem solving: (a) reading the problem for understanding; (b) paraphrasing and visualizing the problem or representing the problem; (c) developing a hypothesis or solution plan; (d) estimating the answer; and (e) computing and checking the problem for accuracy (Montague, 2002). Reading the problem implies understanding the problem parts and establishing relationships among the parts. Paraphrasing is a representation process that requires translation of the linguistic information in the problem by rephrasing or restating the problem in one's own words. Visualization is another representation process that shows the relationships among the problem components. Students can be taught to develop schematic representations, using manipulatives, pencil and paper, or by making mental images. The reading and representation processes help problem solvers develop a solution hypothesis that is directly linked to their "sense-making." Estimation helps students in goal-setting and validation of their plan and solution. Computation involves both declarative and procedural knowledge, and checking involves working backwards to ensure that the problem-solving process as well as the answer is correct. Metacognitive strategies enable the learner to exercise self-regulation while engaged in problem solving. Problem solvers use these strategies to tell themselves what to do (self-instruction), ask themselves questions (self-questioning), and monitor their performance (self-checking).

Teachers need to be able to demonstrate and model the use of these processes and strategies, so that students with learning problems understand how good problem solvers think. Verbalizing or talking aloud when students are first learning how to solve mathematical problems helps students to internalize the processes and strategies. Consider the following demonstration by Mr. Wright, an upper elementary mathematics teacher. He is working with a small group of five students who need explicit instruction in how to solve Division problems before they can fully participate in the mathematics class. Mr. Wright consciously engages in process modeling by saying aloud everything he is thinking and doing as he solves the following problem using an overhead projector so he can also demonstrate what he does.

The class is having a play in the school gym. There are 276 chairs. The teacher wants the children to arrange the chairs in rows with 12 chairs in each row. How many rows will there be?

Mr. Wright: What does a good problem solver do to solve this problem? I will demonstrate how a good problem solver would approach this problem. I am going to think out loud as I solve the problem. That is, I am going to say everything I am thinking and doing.

First, I need to READ the problem for understanding. So, I will say to myself—Read the problem. The class is having a play in the school gym. There are 276 chairs. The teacher wants the children to arrange the chairs in rows with 12 chairs in each row. How many rows will there be? If I don't understand it, read it again. Now I will ask myself—Have I read and understood the problem? Hmm! I think I need to read the last part again. There are 276 chairs. The teacher wants the children to arrange the chairs in rows with 12 chairs in each row. How many rows will there be? Now I will check myself by checking for understanding as I solve the problem.

Now I will PARAPHRASE the problem. I will say to myself, put the problem into my own words. Okay. We have 276 chairs and need to make rows of 12 chairs each. How many rows? I will underline 276 chairs and 12 chairs in each row. Now I will ask myself—Have I underlined the important information? Yes. Okay, what is the question? How many rows will there be? What am I looking for? The total number of rows if each row has 12 chairs in it. Now I will check myself by checking that the information goes with the question, 276 chairs and 12 chairs in each row. Yes, that is the important information.

Next, I will VISUALIZE the problem by telling myself to make a drawing or a diagram that shows how the information is related. I will make one row of 12 chairs and then another under that. Then I will write 12 under that and add them: $12 + 12 + 12 = 36$.

Okay, another 12 = 48. I still have a long way to go. If I draw 276 chairs, I could circle each group of 12 and find out that way, too. Okay, I ask myself—Does the picture fit the problem? Yes, if I draw all of the chairs, that is 276, I can divide those into groups of 12 chairs each. I think I know what to do. Now I will check myself by checking the picture against the problem information. Let me see. I have all the important information and the picture shows how the parts are related.

Next I have to HYPOTHESIZE or set up a plan to solve the problem. So I say to myself, decide how many steps and operations are needed. Well, it is pretty clear that I need to divide 276 by 12 to get the number of rows. I will write the operation symbol for division. Now I will ask myself—If I divide 276 chairs by 12, how many rows will I have? Now I will ask myself, how many steps are needed? This is a one-step problem. Now I will check myself by checking that the plan makes sense. If it does not, I will ask for help. I do not need help. The plan makes sense.

Okay, then I will ESTIMATE or predict the answer. I will say to myself, round the numbers, do the problem in my head, and write the estimate. Well, 276 is close to 300 and 12 is close to 10. Three hundred divided by 10 equals 30. Now I will write the estimate. There, my answer should be about 30 rows. Now I will ask myself—Did I round up and down? Yes, I rounded up and down. Did I write the estimate? Yes. Now I will check myself by checking that I used the important information. Yes, I used all of the important information.

Okay, I am ready to COMPUTE, that is, to do the arithmetic. I will say to myself—Do the operations in the right order. Two hundred seventy-six divided by 12; 12 into 2, no, 12 into 27, twice, 2 × 12 equals 24, put a 2 above the 7 and write 24 below. Subtract 24 from 27 for 3 and bring down the 6. Start over. Thirty-six divided by 12 goes…let me see…12, 24, 36…three times. Put a 3 over the 6, and the answer is 23 rows. Now I will ask myself—How does my answer compare with my estimate? It's not far from 30. Does my answer make sense? Yes, it does. Are the decimals or money signs in the right order? None needed. Now I will check myself by checking that all the operations were done in the right order. Only one. Division. Okay.

Now, finally, I will CHECK to make sure everything is right. So, I will say to myself—Check the computation. Hmm, I can use the reverse operation. 23 × 12 = 276. It's right. I will ask myself—Have I checked every step? Yes, I have. Have I used the right numbers? Twelve, 276, yes. Have I checked the computation? Yes. Just to make sure, I will use my calculator to divide and then to check my answer. Is my answer right? Yes. Now I will check myself by checking that everything is right. If not, I will go back. Then I will ask for help if I need it. But I do not need help. I did it right.

Teaching this cognitive/metacognitive problem-solving process to students with LD requires a systematic approach and proven instructional procedures (see Montague, 2002). The following section presents several principles and procedures that have been effective with students who have difficulty solving mathematical word problems.

Instructional Principles and Procedures

An explicit instructional approach is recommended for teaching students processes and strategies for effective problem solving. Explicit instruction incorporates validated instructional principles and procedures including cueing, modeling, rehearsal, distributed practice, corrective feedback, positive reinforcement, overlearning, and mastery. With this approach, students learn how to be active participants as they engage in problem solving, how to communicate with their teachers and classmates about the problems they solve, and how to be independent and confident when they solve problems. Most students have intact processes and have acquired naturally a set of strategies that help them solve problems. A constructivist classroom environment enhances the knowledge and skills that these students bring to the experience. In contrast, students with LD need intensive but short-term instruction to acquire or activate these processes and strategies. Then they can participate more fully alongside their peers in these problem-solving experiences. As they become more familiar with these necessary cognitive and metacognitive tools and become more successful problem solvers, their motivation and confidence will improve as well.

Cueing can take a variety of forms. Master-class charts that list the problem-solving processes and strategies can be displayed in the classroom. Students can also carry individual cue cards with them as reminders. Teachers can cue students either auditorially or visually to respond when appropriate. At the outset, teachers are the models for students. As soon as students learn the problem-solving process, they can become the models for other students. They gain confidence as they are able to talk through the problem-solving process. When students are first learning the processes and strategies, it is important that they memorize and verbalize them daily. They need to know that problem solving involves reading the problem with understanding, representing the problem by paraphrasing it and then making a visual representation, developing a hypothesis for solving the problem, estimating the answer, and then computing and checking the problem. They also need to be taught when and how to ask for help. When students have learned the process and are comfortable solving problems, they need distributed practice, corrective feedback, and positive reinforcement to ensure that they are automatic in their responses. Automaticity is a result of overlearning and integration of learning within the cognitive system. Only when students are able to function at the automatic level can we say that they have truly learned and mastered a concept, strategy, or skill.

SUMMARY

We know that Division is a complex mathematical procedure that requires understanding of all of the other mathematical operations. However, we know very little specifically about the cognitive processes that underlie Division. Learning the traditional Division algorithm is a challenge for many children, but it often is an insurmountable task for students with LD. When Division is a required operation in a mathematical word problem, the only recourse for many of these students simply is to give up. If students with LD are taught the necessary mathematical concepts and skills as well as the social–interpersonal behaviors important for success in a reform-based constructivist mathematics classroom, they should have a greater chance of being exposed to higher level thinking and learning more in a stimulating mathematical environment.

REFERENCES

Baxter, J., Woodward, J., Voorhies, J., & Wong, J. (2002). We talk about it, but do they get it? *Learning Disabilities Research & Practice, 17,* 173–185.

Bley, N. S., & Thornton, C. A. (1995). *Teaching mathematics to students with LD.* Austin, TX: Pro-Ed.

Burton, G. M. (1992). Young children's choices of manipulatives and strategies for solving whole number division problems. *Focus on Learning Problems in Mathematics, 14,* 2–17.

Cawley, J. F., Fitzmaurice-Hayes, A. M., & Shaw, R. A. (1988). *Mathematics for the mildly handicapped: A guide to curriculum and instruction.* Boston: Allyn & Bacon.

Foley, T. E., & Cawley, J. F. (2003). About the mathematics of division: Implications for students with disabilities. *Exceptionality, 11,* 131–149.

Geary, D. C. (1994). *Children's mathematical development.* Washington, DC: American Psychological Association.

Jitendra, A., DiPipi, C. M., & Perron-Jones, N. (2002). An exploratory study of schema-based word-problem-solving instruction for middle school students with LD: An emphasis on conceptual and procedural understanding. *The Journal of Special Education, 36,* 23–38.

Li, Y., & Silver, E. A. (2000). Can younger students succeed where older students fail? An examination of third graders' solutions of a division-with-remainder (DWR) problem. *Journal of Mathematical Behavior, 19,* 233–246.

Maccini, P., & Gagnon, J. C. (2002). Perceptions and application of NCTM standards by special and general education teachers. *Exceptional Children, 68,* 325–344.

Montague, M. (1996). What does the "new view" of school mathematics mean for students with mild disabilities? In M. Pugach & C. Warger (Eds.), *Curriculum trends, special education, and reform: Refocusing the conversation* (pp. 84–93). New York: Teachers College Press.

Montague, M. (2002). *Solve It! A practical approach for teaching mathematical problem solving.* Reston, VA: Exceptional Innovations.

Montague, M., & Applegate, B. (2001). Middle school students' perceptions, persistence, and performance in mathematical problem solving. *Learning Disability Quarterly, 23,* 215–228.

National Council of Teachers of Mathematics. (1989). *Curriculum and evaluation NCTM standards for school mathematics.* Reston, VA: NCTM.

National Council of Teachers of Mathematics. (2000). *Principles and NCTM standards for school mathematics.* Reston, VA: NCTM.

Silver, E. A. (1992). Referential mappings and the solution of division story problems involving remainders. *Focus on Learning Problems in Mathematics, 14,* 29–39.

Woodward, J., & Montague, M. (2002). Meeting the challenge of mathematics reform for students with LD. *The Journal of Special Education, 36,* 89–101.

Understanding the Concept of "Division": Assessment Considerations

Rene S. Parmar

Department of Administrative and Instructional Leadership
St. John's University

This article presents a summary of considerations for teachers when assessing a student's understanding of Division concepts. As with all mathematical concepts, children develop a basic idea of Division through interactions with others in daily life, beginning from the preschool years. As they move into elementary school, Division is introduced as an arithmetic operation, building on their prior knowledge of addition, subtraction, and multiplication. As children advance to middle school, various uses of fractional concepts are introduced, along with algorithms involving rational numbers. Although there is no clear demarcation as to the grade at which a more advanced level of understanding may be taught, for the purpose of discussion, this article is organized into three broad levels: Preschool, Elementary, and Middle School. Within each level, the assessment of (a) student products, (b) student procedures and strategies, and (c) student concepts and explanations, is presented. Examples of assessment activities and examples of possible student misconceptions are provided. The article concludes with a discussion of the assessment of teaching practices using Division as a model for other areas of mathematics.

Within the area of numbers and operations, the National Council of Teachers of Mathematics (NCTM) stresses that children need to be aware of understanding numbers, ways of representing numbers, relationships among numbers, and number systems (NCTM, 2000, p. 33). With reference to the concept of "Division," NCTM Standards state that children need to learn how to understand and represent fractions in context. The Standards provide the basis for a broad conceptualization of "Division," beginning as an understanding of partition in the early years, and progressing to a sophisticated understanding of the many applications of rational numbers by the end of middle school.

Standardized tests have been widely used for assessment of general learning disabilities and specific mathematical learning disabilities. The available standardized instruments typically rate students as passing (providing a correct answer) or failing (providing an incorrect

Requests for reprints should be sent to Rene S. Parmar, Department of Administrative and Instructional Leadership, St. John's University, 8000 Utopia Parkway, Queens, NY 11439. E-mail: parmarr@stjohns.edu answer) items that cover various skill areas and problem solving in mathematics. They provide information on the relative standing of students in comparison to their age-peers. Some instruments provide some diagnostic information through error analyses of student responses, but these are rare. Many standardized instruments have strong psychometric properties, but may be weak in the area of content (Parmar, Cawley, & Frazita, 1996). As a supplement to standardized tests, Bryant and Rivera (1997) have suggested several alternative modes of assessment, including the use of portfolios, error analyses based on word problems, interviews with students, and observations.

For the purposes of instructionally useful assessment, it is important to go beyond simply evaluating whether a student's response is correct or incorrect. In fact, when conducting assessment, a teacher should use only a small number of items, each of which has been carefully selected to represent various critical aspects of understanding. In this article, it is recommended that the assessment data that are collected should include three important dimensions:

1. *Observations* of the students' actions while they are engaged in problem solving that can reveal their strategy knowledge and use. These observations may be brief, such as a checklist of strategies, or longer narratives.
2. A record of the students' *responses* or answers or physical products (e.g., drawings, displays) that can be used for error analysis.
3. Students' *explanations* of their reasoning processes, that reveal their conceptual knowledge and the connections they make among various mathematical concepts and procedures. These include explanations in any form (graphic, symbolic, verbal, written).

While the aforementioned three dimensions are certainly more time consuming than the traditional paper-and-pencil unit test, they are well worth the effort for several reasons. First, the students we are concerned with are already experiencing difficulty in school and possible failure in mathematics. Simply telling them that their performance continues to remain poor does not lead to improvement. Second, if students do not develop a good understanding of basic concepts in the early years of school they will either continue to learn erroneously or discontinue learning in later grades. Effective assessment is essential if a teacher is to modify curriculum and instructional practice to address students' specialized learning needs. Third, comprehensive and effective assessment is a means of feedback, to the teacher, as to whether he or she is (a) covering the important concepts within a topic, and (b) using teaching strategies that are building the conceptual understanding of students. Using the above ideas, suggestions for the assessment of Division are discussed below.

ASSESSMENT OF DIVISION CONCEPTS IN THE PRESCHOOL YEARS

Preschool children initially conceptualize division in the context of sharing, using a "partitive schema." Young children have been observed to be adept at making fair shares between two and three persons (Frydman & Bryant, 1988), and even to be able to calculate fractional amounts less than or equal to one (Mix, Levine, & Huttenlocher, 1999). In sharing among several people (dividing into groups), children may be able to equally divide groups of discrete objects even before they attain fluency in counting (Steffe & Cobb, 1983).

Researchers have also investigated the "quotitive schema" (i.e., if each person gets a certain quota, how many people can share a given amount), and posited that concepts such as repeated subtraction may form the basis for understanding this aspect of division (Fischbein, Deri, Nello, & Marino, 1985), although quotition is more difficult than partition at this age.

At the preschool level, assessment of the Division concept incorporates three critical aspects. First, there is the understanding of the inverse relationship between the number of shares and the size of each share. Second, there is the numeric dimension where children use either counting or a basic knowledge of addition and subtraction to arrive at a solution. Third, there is comprehension of specialized vocabulary that is associated with using Division in story or everyday contexts. Figure 1 presents some illustrative items that incorporate the three aspects, also incorporating modes of presentation that are appropriate for this age level. Teachers may vary the context to make the items more relevant to their specific group of students, or may incorporate more

---

Inverse Relationship Between Number of Shares and Size of Share

    (a) Contrasting Totals

    I have this cup of raisins (point to a large cup full of raisins) and this cup of raisins (point to a small cup of raisins). I can share the first one among 3 children (put contents of large cup onto three small plates). [Clear the raisins away]. Or I can share the other one among 3 children (put contents of small cup onto three small plates). [Clear the raisins away]. Did the 3 children get more from the first cup or the second?

    (b) Contrasting Recipients

    I have a cup full of raisins. I can share it among 3 children (put onto three small plates). [Pour the raisins back into the cup]. Or I can share it among 5 children (put onto five small plates). Which group of children will get more?

Use of Quantity and Number (Manipulative Format)

    (a) Partitive: I want to give four girls equal parts of this straw. Show me how I can cut it up for them. Quotitive: I'm going to share this cookie among the children (cut up a circle into quadrants). How many children will get a piece?

    (b) Partitive: Here are six chips to share among three children. How many chips will each child get? Quotitive: I have eight chips and want to give each child two chips. How many children will get chips?

Special Vocabulary

Numeric: half, thirds, fourths, quarter

Distributive: equal, each, share, pieces

FIGURE 1   Sample Division items for preschool students.

abstract modes of representation, such as presenting items verbally without manipulatives or pictures.

Examples of actions, responses, and explanations that are reflective of an incorrect or incomplete understanding of Division concepts are presented here.

Preschool Children's Procedures (Actions)

1. Counting errors. In the preschool years, children are not always consistent in counting, and any changes in the arrangement of objects (e.g., from a linear display to a randomly grouped display) may lead to confusion.
2. Losing track of who received a share. Children may give one person an additional share or skip a recipient.
3. Difficulties with reading the symbols, if an item is presented in a display or written format (Mix et al., 1999).
4. Difficulties with vocabulary and terminology, such as the meaning of "equal" shares and "each" person receiving a share.

Preschool Children's Products (Answers)

1. Picking the largest one. Children may be observed to select the visually largest amount and state that amount as an answer (related to the conservation of quantity, noted by Piaget (Derr, 1985).
2. Giving a related, but nonmathematical answer. Children may state, "It's not fair!" when presented with a problem where some children get a larger share than others.

Preschool Children's Concepts (Explanations)

1. Difficulty with the idea of equal, or fair, shares.
2. Overgeneralization of rules that apply to whole numbers (e.g., one fourth is greater than one third because 4 is greater than 3) (Sophian, Garyantes, & Chang, 1997).
3. Difficulty with the concept that a number may refer not to specific objects, as in counting, but rather to sets or groups (Clark & Kamii, 1996).
4. Difficulty in dealing with two numbers, the number of shares (numerator) and the size of each share (denominator) (Gallistel & Gelman, 1992).
5. Difficulty in visualizing objects arranging into patterns or arrays, which would facilitate partition into equal groups (McClain & Cobb, 1999), or constructing a representation based on irrelevant attributes such as color or texture (Mix et al., 1999).
6. Difficulty in keeping track of items as they move into and out of a space (a whole set being divided or recombined), especially if the items are rotated or the layout is reorganized (Mix et al., 1999).

For the purposes of ongoing evaluation and communication with parents, teachers may use a rubric to track the level of understanding of young children, and make instructional decisions. For example, the following rubric, adapted from Correa, Bryant, & Nunes (1998) can be a useful tool.

Level 1: No valid justification (random responses, descriptions of materials)
Level 2: Qualitative judgment ("they have the same so they won't fight"; "it's fair")
Level 3: Some constituents of sharing (each person got [a given number])
Level 4: Seeing numeric relationships (e.g., 4 girls and 12 flowers, so each gets 3)
Level 5: Inverse divisor—quotient relationship (if there are more people, each will get less; if some people don't get any, the others will get more).

ASSESSMENT OF DIVISION CONCEPTS IN THE ELEMENTARY GRADES

At the elementary level, two types of Division word problems are typically included in the curriculum. These are (a) *equal groups*, related to the concepts of repeated subtraction and rates; and (b) *Division comparison*, where two sets are involved and one set consists of multiple copies of the other (Van de Walle, 2001) (presented in Figure 2a). Difficulties with word problems, particularly those with more than one step, have been identified as among the chief concerns of teachers who teach mathematics to children with learning disabilities (Bryant, Bryant, & Hammill, 2000).

In the early elementary grades children use their knowledge of partition of whole numbers to solve fraction problems through determination of common denominators for addition and subtraction of fractions (Mack, 1995). In this context, children need to understand that a fraction is a relative quantity, dependent on a referent (whole). Therefore a given fraction can represent very different actual quantities. Assessment may include asking children to draw and explain various representations of various fractional parts, as illustrated for "half" in Figure 2b.

Elementary School Children's Procedures (Actions)

1. Use of incorrect or inefficient strategies. Figure 2c is a listing of strategies for division, and teachers can use this chart to determine a student's current strategy and move them to a more effective one. As observed with other operations (Geary, Brown, & Samaranayake, 1991), children with mathematical disabilities often use less mature strategies than their age peers, and have more difficulty retrieving an efficient strategy, even when it has been taught to them.

2. Difficulties with Division notation. There are three symbolic notations for writing out Division problems that are commonly found in school textbooks. The first, a ÷ b, is based on the common convention for a number sentence as used for other operations, and most closely maps the way Division is stated and conceptualized. The second type of notation, a/b, requires the use of a specialized understanding where the top term is

Construct	Type of Division	Sample Item
Equal Groups	Partition (fair sharing) size of the sets is unknown	Mala has eight candy bars. She wants to share them among her four brothers. How many will each brother receive?
	Quotition (measurement or repeated subtraction) number of groups is unknown	Mala has eight candy bars. She gave each of her brothers two. How many brothers does she have?
Division Comparison	Partition (fair sharing) the size of one set is unknown, and must be determined based on the size of the other	Mala had eight candy bars yesterday. Today she has half as many. How many candy bars does she have today?
	Quotition (measurement or repeated subtraction) one set is a particular multiple of the other	Mala saved money from her allowance. Each week she saved five cents. How many weeks did it take her to save 35 cents?

FIGURE 2a   Sample Division items for elementary school students.

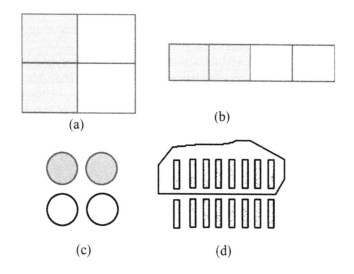

(a)

(b)

(c)   (d)

Contexts for the Concept of "Half."
(a) Nina watered half the lawn.
(b) Nina walked half the distance.
(c) Nina had four cupcakes and ate half.
(d) Half the children went on the field trip.

FIGURE 2b

Sample Item: Nina wants to share treats equally among her 3 kittens. She has 15 treats. How many will each kitten get?

Type of Strategy	Description	Example
Direct Counting	Physical materials are used to model problem, and objects are counted to obtain result	1, 1, 1; 2, 2, 2; 3, 3, 3; etc.
Rhythmic Counting	Counting follows the structure of the problem; number of sets are simultaneously counted as well	1, 2, 3 (1 round); 1, 2, 3 (2 rounds); etc.
Skip Counting	Counting is done in multiples. It is easier to keep track of the number of groups	3; 6; 9; etc.
Additive Calculation	Counting is replaced by calculation, such as repeated subtraction	15 - 3; 12 - 3; etc.
Multiplicative Calculation	Calculations take the form of known facts from memory	15 divided by 3 is 5 (or inverted from a multiplication fact, as 3 times 5 is 15)

FIGURE 2c   Calculation strategies for Division word problems. Adapted from "Young Children's Intuitive Models of Multiplication and Division," by J. T. Mulligan and M. C. Mitchelmore, 1997, *Journal for Research in Mathematics Education, 28,* 309–330.

recognized as the "dividend" or whole quantity, and the lower term as the "divisor," or number of sets or parts. The third type of notation is the most confusing, where the arrangement of the information is inconsistent with the verbalization, as in $b\overline{)a}$. This form is used for paper–pencil computation. Unfortunately, in addition to being inherently confusing, the third form also leads to inappropriate verbal statements regarding division such as "b goes into a," which continue to be observed in classroom teaching practices, despite their discontinuation in textbooks (Van de Walle, 2001). Teachers need to evaluate whether students are correctly reading the terms in each notation, and therefore using the numbers in the correct way to solve a division item.

Elementary School Children's Products (Answers)

1. Incorrect algorithm. Students may invert the dividend and the divisor or make other related errors, which appear to be based on students' rote learning of an algorithm without corresponding understanding.

2. Incorrect statement of response. Students may change responses or numbers within an item to fit their intuitive belief that dividing always results in a smaller number.

3. Incorrect application of principles from other operations. Students may surmise that Division is commutative, since they have previously learned that multiplication is commutative, and that Division is the inverse of multiplication.

4. Incorrect choice of operation. These errors could be related to incorrect reading of the Division symbol, lack of knowledge of division therefore substituting an

operation that is known, or lack of adequate comprehension of the item. This type of error is more frequent with speeded tests, or items in unfamiliar contexts (Campbell, 1997).

5. Incorrect fact retrieval. Students attempt to solve problems based on recollection of multiplication facts, but make errors in recall. For example, 3×6 is recalled as 15 instead of 18.

6. Incomplete understanding of place value and base 10. When working on long-division algorithms in a paper-and-pencil format, children need to constantly attend to the place value of the given numbers to "bring down" the correct number, and align their computation. Children with mathematical disabilities were observed to have difficulty with these concepts even in the early stages of learning arithmetic computation with addition (Jordan & Hanich, 2000), and these difficulties often persist through more advanced topics in arithmetic.

Elementary School Children's Concepts (Explanations)

1. Failure to use arrays as models. When learning addition and subtraction, students use the models of sets and number lines for solving problems. For multiplication and Division, the additional model of arrays is useful in conceptualizing the problem.

2. Difficulty with Division by 0 or 1. This may be related to an incomplete understanding of base 10, and exacerbated by teachers using an incorrect form for Division items, such as the term "goes into." The confusion may be mitigated by using a correct form of questioning, such as "How many groups with x in each group can you make from y?" Here students see that you (a) cannot make groups with 0 in each group, and (b) if you make groups with 1 in each group, the resulting number of groups is the same as the numbers of elements within the group.

3. Difficulty with remainders. In real-life situations, more often than not, Division produces results that are not a whole number. Students with incomplete conceptual understanding of remainders have been observed to engage in three types of incorrect practices (Van de Walle, 2001). These are: (1) the remainder is ignored, and a whole-number answer is stated; (2) the remainder is interpreted to be equal to a set, and added to the answer; or (3) the answer is rounded to the nearest whole number for an approximate result.

ASSESSMENT OF DIVISION CONCEPTS IN MIDDLE SCHOOL

In middle school, the focus moves to using rational numbers. Here children understand the idea that many things cannot be evenly divided using whole numbers, and that rational numbers provide a way of representing this fact (e.g., 3 cookies divided among 4 children gives each three fourth of a cookie). The NCTM Standards for the middle grades include the understanding of different numerical forms (whole numbers, fractions, decimals and percents), the ability to translate between the various forms, and their relationships (NCTM, 2000). The concept of fractions can be viewed in a variety of contexts, such as area (partitioning squares and circles), quantity (partitioning sets or shares of objects), and lines (partitioning the number line and using fraction strips). Representations can be in a graphic, numeric, symbolic, or linguistic modes (Gearhart, et al., 1999).

Some mathematics educators have decried the practice on focusing only on the part-whole concept of rational numbers in the middle-school years (Lamon, 2001), noting that there are at least five different ways in which rational numbers are applied at this level (Figure 3). Rather than focusing on just memorizing algorithms for fractional computation, children need to be brought to an understanding of the five applications, and the connections among them.

Middle School Children's Procedures (Actions)

1. Confusion with vocabulary. An incorrect understanding of what is the "denominator" or the "numerator" can lead to errors. Students can also confuse terms such as "one fifth" with their previous understanding of cardinality (fifth).

2. Difficulty with identifying the whole unit to be divided, especially when the whole in a given item could be a part in another (e.g., dividing a box of cookies, and dividing a single cookie).

Rational Number Interpretation of 5/6	Description	Example
Part/Whole	5 parts out of 6 equal parts	Draw 3 different representations of 5 out of 6, using cupcakes as a unit of measurement. 5 (cupcakes) = 10 (half cupcakes) 6 (cupcakes) = 12 (half cupcakes)
Operator	5/6 of something (divide by 6 and multiply by 5)	If a girl loses 5/6 of 30 marbles, how many has she lost? $(30 \div 6) \times 5 = (5) \times 5 = 25$
Ratios and Rates	5 parts to 6 parts per quantity	If each boy gets 5 flowers and each girl gets flowers, what is the ratio of flowers among the boys and girls? How many flowers will the girls have if there are 3 boys? 5:6 $(3)5 : (3)6 = 15:18$
Quotient	5 divided by 6 (5/6)	If 6 girls share 5 sandwiches how much does each girl get? 5/6
Measure	5 (one-sixth units)	Everyone has 1/6 of a box of raisins; how much do 5 people have together? 5(1/6)

Note. The five types of Division constructs are derived from "Presenting and Representing: From Fractions to Rational Numbers," by S. Lamon in *The Roles of Representation in School Mathematics: 2001* yearbook, A. A. Louco and F. R. Curcio (Eds.), 2001. Reston, VA: NCTM, pp.146–165.

FIGURE 3   Sample Division items for middle school students.

Middle School Children's Products (Answers)

1. Difficulty with the meaning of numerator and denominator, where the numerator represents the count (how many shares or parts) and the denominator represents the size of the share.

2. Difficulty moving from one fraction representation to another (e.g., $1/5 = 20\% = .20$).

3. Inaccurate recall of number facts, leading to errors.

4. Inaccurate use of subtraction or addition, when using a traditional paper–pencil division algorithm. Teachers must be aware that incorrect responses can be the result of inaccuracies in operations other than division, and therefore work on correcting the source of the error.

Middle School Children's Concepts (Explanations)

1. Incorrect mental models. When solving problems based on fractions, children may conceptualize the problem using one of three basic models: (a) the regional or area model, (b) the length or measurement model, and (c) the set model, including the use of arrays (Van de Walle, 2001). Figure 2b illustrates the models, using the concept of "Half." Use of an incorrect conceptualization or model will lead to errors.

To assess how children construct models when given problems, teachers may use a variety of commercially available materials to set up problem situations, asking students to identify various fractional parts (e.g., $3/7$, $12/17$). For the regional model, pattern blocks, grid (graph) paper, geoboards, or folded sheets of paper may be used to ask children to partition into pieces. For the length model, Cuisenaire rods, line-segment drawings, fraction strips, or folded strips of paper may be used. For the set model, counters or other small manipulatives, or marks on paper may be used.

2. Difficulty understanding that there may be an infinite number of values between any two given fractional numbers.

ASSESSMENT OF TEACHING PRACTICES

The development of students' understanding of Division, or any concept in mathematics, is closely related to their experiences learning that concept. We have advocated in the past that special-education teachers be aware of learning standards recommended by professional organizations, and curriculum frameworks from general education that apply to students with learning disabilities (Parmar & Cawley, 1997).

Research has demonstrated that there is a significant positive correlation between teachers' knowledge of students' problem solving (Peterson, Carpenter, & Fennema, 1989). Further, there appears to be a significant negative effect of teachers' relying solely on student written answers for assessment.

1. Calculate the following:

$\frac{1}{4} \div 4 =$

$\frac{1}{4} \div 3/5 =$

$4 \div \frac{1}{4} =$

$320 \div 1/3 =$

2. Write an expression that will solve the following problems:

(1) A five-meter stick was divided into 15 equal sticks. What is the length of each stick?
(2) Four friends bought $\frac{1}{4}$ kg of chocolate and shared it equally. How much did each friend get?
(3) Four kg of cheese were packed in packages of $\frac{1}{4}$ kg each. How many packages contained this amount of cheese?

Note. From "Enhancing Prospective Teachers" Knowledge of Children's Conceptions: The Case of Division of Fractions," by D. Tirosh, 2000, *Journal for Research in Mathematics Education, 31,* 5–25.

FIGURE 4   A sample teacher self-assessment for Division.

Prior to undertaking instruction in Division, teachers need to identify and understand the basic and higher level concepts they are trying to teach. As Tirosh (2000) describes, teachers may themselves hold erroneous views of Division concepts and procedures. As a self-assessment, teachers may undertake to respond to Division items (as illustrated in Figure 4), through (a) deriving an answer, (b) stating possible incorrect answers, and (c) identifying potential sources of student errors. By sharing responses with other teachers, both in special and general education across various grade levels, a teacher could gain a wealth of information that can be applied to improving instructional design and delivery. Not only should assessment be frequent, but it should be more visible, and paired with immediate feedback, so that all students in the classroom can benefit by identifying common sources of error and ways to circumvent them (Perry, VanderStoep, & Yu, 1993).

CONCLUSIONS

As is evident from the earlier discussion, assessment is a complex process, and should incorporate many aspects of the students' actions, answers, and explanations, as well as the teaching process. In this article, Division is used as an illustration of the various dimensions of mathematical learning incorporated within computation. The ideas may be extended to addition, subtraction, and multiplication as well. The items presented for discussion may be modified to fit the context of the child and classroom where the assessment is to take place.

Teachers should constantly emphasize conceptual understanding, based on an in-depth assessment process, rather than simple assessment of procedures and algorithms.

Instead of repeatedly failing students for providing incorrect answers, it is worthwhile to discover the source of the error and use that information as the basis for good instructional practice.

REFERENCES

Bryant, B. R., & Rivera, D. P. (1997). Educational assessment of mathematics skills and abilities. *Journal of Learning Disabilities, 30,* 57–68.

Bryant, D. P., Bryant, B. R., & Hammill, D. (2000). Characteristic behaviors of students with LD who have teacher-identified math weaknesses. *Journal of Learning Disabilities, 33,* 168–178.

Campbell, J. I. D. (1997). On the relation between skilled performance of simple division and multiplication. *Journal of Experimental Psychology: Learning, Memory, & Cognition, 23,* 1140–1159.

Clark, F. B., & Kamii, C. (1996). Identification of multiplicative thinking in children in grades 1–5. *Journal for Research in Mathematics Education, 27,* 41–51.

Correa, J., Bryant, P., & Nunes, T. (1998). Young children's understanding of division: The relationship between division terms in a noncomputational task. *Journal of Educational Psychology, 90,* 321–330.

Derr, A. (1985). Conservation and mathematics achievement in the learning disabled child. *Journal of Learning Disabilities, 18,* 333–336.

Fischbein, E., Deri, M., & Nello, M. S. (1985). The role of implicit models in solving verbal problems in multiplication and division. *Journal for Research in Mathematics Education, 16,* 3–17.

Frydman, O., & Bryant, P. (1988). Sharing and the understanding of number equivalence by young children. *Cognitive Development, 3,* 323–339.

Gallistel, C. R., & Gelman, R. (1992). Preverbal and verbal counting and computation. *Cognition, 44,* 48–74.

Gearhart, M., Saxe, G. B., Seltzer, J., Schlackman, J., Ching, C. C., Nasir, N., Fall, R., Bennett, T., Rhine, S., & Sloan, T. (1999). Opportunities to learn fractions in elementary mathematics classrooms. *Journal for Research in Mathematics Education, 30,* 286–315.

Geary, D. C., Brown, S. C., & Samaranayake, V. A. (1991). Cognitive addition: A short longitudinal study of strategy choice and speed-of-processing differences in normal and mathematics disabled children. *Developmental Psychology, 27,* 787–797.

Jordan, N. C., & Hanich, L. B. (2000). Mathematical thinking in second-grade children with different forms of LD. *Journal of Learning Disabilities, 33,* 567–578.

Lamon, S. (2001). Presenting and representing: From fractons to rational numbers. In A. A. Couco & F. R. Curcio (Eds.), *The roles of representation in school mathematics: 2001 yearbook* (pp. 146–165). Reston, VA: NCTM.

Mack, N. K. (1995). Confounding whole-number and fraction concepts when building on informal knowledge. *Journal for Research in Mathematics Education, 26,* 422–441.

McClain, K., & Cobb, P. (1998). Supporting students' ways of reasoning about patterns and partitions. In J. Copely (Ed.), *Mathematics in the early years* (pp. 112–118). Reston, VA: NCTM.

Mix, K. S., Levine, S. C., & Huttenlocher, J. (1999). Early fraction calculation ability. *Developmental Psychology, 35,* 164–174.

Mulligan, J. T., & Mitchelmore, M. C. (1997). Young children's intuitive models of multiplication and division. *Journal for Research in Mathematics Education, 28,* 309–330.

National Council of Teachers of Mathematics. (2000). *Principles and standards for school mathematics.* Reston, VA: Author.

Parmar, R. S., & Cawley, J. F. (1997). Preparing teachers to teach mathematics to students with learning disabilities. *Journal of Learning Disabilities, 30,* 188–197.

Parmar, R. S., Cawley, J. F., & Frazita, R. (1996). Mathematics assessment for students with mild disabilities: An exploration of content validity. *Learning Disability Quarterly, 19*(2), 127–136.

Perry, M., VanderStoep, S. W., & Yu, S. L. (1993). Asking questions in first-grade mathematics classes: Potential influences in mathematical thought. *Journal of Educational Psychology, 85,* 31–40.

Peterson, P. L., Carpenter, T., & Fennema, E. (1989). Teachers' knowledge of students' knowledge in mathematics problem solving: Correlational and case analysis. *Journal of Educational Psychology, 81,* 558–569.

Sophian, C., Garyantes, D., & Chang, C. (1997). When three is less than two: Early developments in children's understanding of fractional quantities. *Developmental Psychology, 33,* 731–744.

Steffe, L. P., & Cobb, P. (1983). Cognitive development and children's solutions to verbal arithmetic problems: A critique. *Journal for Research in Mathematics Education, 14,* 74–76.

Tirosh, D. (2000). Enhancing prospective teachers' knowledge of children's conceptions: The case of division of fractions. *Journal for Research in Mathematics Education, 31,* 5–25.

Van de Walle, J. A. (2001). *Elementary and middle school mathematics: Teaching developmentally* (4th ed.). New York: Longman.